365

WILD GAME RECIPES

EDIE FRANSON

Published by

 **krause
publications**

700 E. State Street • Iola, WI 54990-0001
Telephone: 715/445-2214
www.krause.com

Please call or write for our free catalog of publications.
Our toll-free number to place an order or obtain a free catalog is 800-258-0929 or
please use our regular business telephone, 715-445-2214.

Library of Congress Catalog Number: 2001090664
ISBN: 0-87341-995-2

Printed in the United States of America

Dedication

For my husband, Jim.
I couldn't have done this without you.

Contents

Acknowledgments

As with any book, the accomplishment could not be completed without the encouragement, support, and assistance of one's family and friends. They contributed their time and effort in helping make my dream, this book, a reality.

Special people deserve mentioning. Terri Fisher and Lori Writz, my daughters, who both spent endless hours proofreading, analyzing, and making suggestions. Daughter-in-law, Amy, whose faith in me that I could do this kept me going. Sons, Lonn and Kyle Franson for their hunting and fishing expertise in supplying some of the game and fish for recipe experimentation. Son-in-law, Mike Writz, who enthusiastically sampled the experiments, and son-in-law, Greg Fisher, the computer expert, who saved me when I had major computer glitches.

My grateful thanks to those who shared suggestions and recipes. They include Sally and Scott Willman, Dr. Eric and Jackie Swanson, Sue Hannam, Peggy Hayes, Rita Carlson, and Elizabeth Martin.

I also owe a debt of thanks to my mother-in-law, Agnes Franson. A number of years ago, she was the first person to share her wild rice recipe with a new bride, that has led that bride to this point in time.

And finally, my thanks to all those who said at some time or another, "you should write a book with all your recipes." This is for you.....enjoy!

Foreword

It's difficult to summarize the hunting and fishing experience because its appeal holds so many facets.

Consider Oct. 1, 1998, when I joined Edie Franson and her husband, Jim, for a day of ruffed grouse hunting at their beautiful northeastern Wisconsin property. A still, frosty dawn gave way to brilliant autumn day as Magnum, the Fransons' veteran golden retriever, and Belle, my 11-month-old black Labrador, quartered through golden aspens and black spruce. At noon, with two grouse in our game bags, we broke for a luxurious field lunch under a colorful hardwood canopy. That evening, with three more grouse in hand, we relaxed, tired dogs at our feet, as Edie prepared what turned out to be the finest grouse dinner I've experienced.

Since then, I've been privileged to share a fishing boat with Jim and his son, Lonn, and have worked and hunted ducks with Kyle, the other Franson boy. And as I learned that October day, they're truly folks who live and cherish the outdoors lifestyle.

That has always come through in Edie's writing and recipes. She and I came to *Wisconsin Outdoor Journal* at about the same time; I was the new editor, and Edie was the new "Camp Cook" columnist. Almost seven years, 40-plus issues and probably more than 100 recipes later, I'm still amazed at the depth and substance of her work. If a walleye recipe appears in "Camp Cook," you can bet that fish was hooked, landed, cleaned, cooked and polished off by the Franson clan. Likewise, any venison recipe probably stems from a buck born, raised, shot, dressed and consumed on the Fransons' home ground.

Accordingly, I think it's no coincidence that "Camp Cook" has remained one of WOJ's best-read columns and continues to generate the most reader response. Folks seem to sense Edie's zest for the outdoors. And by reading and responding to the column, readers share her love of the experience.

In this cookbook, Edie's first, you'll find more than information on how to fry a walleye or roast a duck. You'll feel a May breeze on your face as you pitch a jig toward the submerged rock pile, and feel the distinct tap before you lean back into a golden-flanked 18-incher. And you'll feel November's chill as you see the greenhead cup his wings and sail into the stiff northwest wind toward your decoys. Better yet, with those experiences fresh in your mind, you'll likely cook up and enjoy the wild-game dinners of your life.

Sunrise, morning dew, lunch afield, an evening deer stand, and succulent fish and game dinners by the campfire; they're all here, in Edie's tasty slice of the outdoors. With luck, this book will be the first of many servings.

Of course, Edie, Jim, Kyle, Lonn and the rest of the Franson family will have to hunt and fish that much more to keep the recipes flowing. But I think they re up to the challenge.

Brian Lovett
Editor, *Wisconsin Outdoor Journal,*
Turkey & Turkey Hunting
March 7, 2001

THE
HEAVYWEIGHTS

A Quick Word about
Cooking the Heavyweights

Originally, the word venison meant the meat of any game – mammal or bird. Today, most people think of it as the meat of all, or at least several, members of the deer family – deer, elk, moose, and caribou. The meat from each animal has its own distinctive flavors, with older animals having a stronger flavor.

The same general cooking rules apply to all big game animals. Game meat is generally cooked the same way as a similar cut of lean beef. I prefer to cook steaks and chops hot and fast. When serving venison, serve it hot and use a heated platter or steak plate.

Some hunters prefer to have a professional butcher cut up their venison. I prefer that it be done at home. When cut up at home, any hair, membrane, blood, fat, and bone fragments left on the meat can be removed. Before starting, consider your family's preferences for steaks, roasts, chops, stew meat, hamburger and sausage and make your cuts accordingly. You are guaranteed to get quality cuts if you do it yourself. Try it! It's not that difficult and is part of the hunting experience.

A general rule of thumb for the number of servings per pound is as follows:

1 pound of boneless meat – 4 servings
1 pound of meat, few bones – 3 servings
1 pound of meat, much bone – 2 servings

If you cut up your own meat, it is advisable to remove as much of the tallow as possible. Since wild game fat becomes rancid quickly, trim it closely. Venison tallow doesn't freeze well and may produce a rancid taste when frozen, even after a couple of months.

What about the bone? Boning out all the meat will provide the best tasting venison. It will also help keep the meat from developing a gamier flavor. Bone marrow is a fatty product and can turn rancid even when frozen. Boned meat wraps easier and takes less freezer space. Boning takes a little bit more time and effort, but the payoff in the end is a meat product that will taste better.

The main consideration in wrapping the cut-up meat is the exclusion of air, which causes drying, also known as freezer burn. If not wrapped properly for freezing, your meat will lose moisture, become dry, tough, and sometimes stringy. It's a good idea to label each package of meat with the animal, type of cut, and date. As an example: Edie's buck, steaks, 11/01. For best flavor, six to eight months is considered maximum keeping time for frozen game. Less is even better.

Ready to use your meat? If possible, thaw the game meat slowly and completely in the refrigerator before cooking. This will help to retain a greater amount of moisture and aid in producing palatable and tender meat.

In general, the principles for domestic meat cookery apply to game cookery. Cooking slowly at low temperature (300 to 325) reduces shrinkage and retains food value and flavor. Methods used vary with tenderness of cut and preferences. The two major methods for cooking meat are dry heat and moist heat. Dry heat is used for roasting, broiling and pan-broiling. Use this method for the tender or tenderized cuts of meat such as the loin and rib cuts. Moist heat is for braising and stewing the less tender cuts or if the animal is extra lean or aged.

As I mentioned previously, the word venison pertains to several members of the deer family. Most of the venison recipes can be made using deer, antelope, elk, or moose.

Bear is also included in this section, even though it is not "venison." The meat is coarser grained than other big game. Young or old, fat or lean, bear meat should be thoroughly cooked so there is no pink tinge to the meat and it reaches an internal temperature of 170 degrees. It is delicious when cooked properly.

Game cookery can be an exciting challenge. It offers a wide variety of meat and the opportunity to try herbs, spices, condiments and vegetables to produce new and interesting flavors. Greater variety in the way you cook game adds to your family's eating pleasure. When cooked properly, the meat is tastier than choice beef.

Bacon Rolled Venison Roast

Great roasted or grilled

2 pounds venison tenderloin
2 tablespoons olive oil
Celery Stuffing (see p.227)
4 to 6 slices bacon
Salt and pepper

Prepare celery stuffing or a stuffing mix of your choice.

Butterfly meat by making a lengthwise cut down center, cutting to within 1/2 inch of the other side, but not through it. Spread open. Cut horizontally, from the center to the outside edge, to within 1/2 inch of the other side of meat. Repeat on opposite side of center. Spread cut sides open to make one thin piece.

Spread olive oil on top side of meat. Sprinkle with salt and pepper. Arrange celery stuffing over top of meat to cover completely. Beginning at the short side, roll up meat. Wrap bacon slices around roll in 4 to 6 places, depending on size of roast. Tie bacon onto roast with heavy string. Sprinkle with salt and pepper, if desired.

To roast in oven, have temperature at 325 degrees. Place rolled roast in a pan; roast for 1 to 1-1/2 hours or until meat is done according to the way you like it.

To grill, have temperature at a medium heat. Place roast in a foil pan. Grill, covered. Proceed with cooking the same as roasting.

To serve, remove string and carve meat into 1/4-inch slices, keeping the spiral effect.

Baked Chili With Wild Rice

1 pound ground venison
2 cups cooked wild rice
1 tablespoon butter or margarine
1 medium onion, chopped
1 can (10-3/4-ounce) tomato soup
1 can (10-3/4-ounce) cream of celery soup
1 can (14-1/2-ounce) chili beans
1 soup can water
Salt and pepper
1/4 teaspoon chili powder

Grease a large casserole dish. In a skillet, melt butter. Sauté onion until tender. Add venison and brown, breaking meat into fine pieces. Cook thoroughly. Drain off any cooking liquid. Place meat and onions into casserole dish. Add in wild rice, both cans of soup, can of water, chili beans, and chili powder. Mix together. Salt and pepper as needed. Cover, bake at 350 degrees for 1 hour.

Variation: Use a Crock-Pot set on low heat and cook for 3 to 4 hours. Follow cooking directions above; omit baking temperature and time.

Barbecue Crock-Pot Venison

2 tablespoons vegetable oil
2 to 3 pounds venison, sliced thin, cut into bite size chunks
Flour, all-purpose
Salt and pepper
2 cans (14-1/2 ounce each) stewed tomatoes
1 cup celery, diced
2 medium onions, chopped
2 green peppers, seeded and chopped
2/3 cup Heinz Thick & Rich Honey barbecue sauce
1/2 cup Heinz 57 sauce
3 teaspoons Worcestershire sauce
4 drops Tabasco sauce

Heat vegetable oil in skillet over medium heat. Combine flour, salt and pepper in a large plastic zip-top bag. Place meat in bag; shake to coat. Brown meat on all sides. Remove meat with a slotted spoon to the Crock-Pot. Add in the stewed tomatoes, celery, onions, peppers, and four sauces. Cook on low for six hours minimum, or on high for three hours, until meat is tender.

Barbecue Venison Meatballs

A tangy appetizer

1 pound ground venison
1/2 pound ground lean pork
1 egg slightly beaten
1/2 cup bread crumbs
1/4 teaspoon sage
1 teaspoon salt
Pepper to taste
1 cup Chili Sauce (see p. 240)
1 tablespoon Worcestershire sauce
2 tablespoons brown sugar
1 tablespoon vinegar

Combine ground venison and pork, beaten egg, bread crumbs, salt and pepper; mix well. Form mixture into 1 inch meatballs. Place in a 9- by 13-inch pan.

Combine chili sauce, Worcestershire sauce, brown sugar, and vinegar and spoon over meatballs. Bake at 325 degrees for approximately 45 to 60 minutes, or until meatballs are completely baked. Baste meatballs with sauce several times during baking.

Black Bear Roast & Vegetables

1 bear roast
1 tablespoon oil
1 can (16-ounce) whole tomatoes, undrained, mashed
1 package dry onion soup mix
Pepper
3 carrots, peeled and sliced
1 can (4-ounce) sliced mushrooms, drained
2 ribs celery, sliced
1 whole bay leaf
Flour, quick-mixing

Heat the oil in a skillet. Braise bear roast on all sides. Remove to roasting pan. Pour tomatoes in skillet, stir in soup mix. Season with pepper. Pour mixture over roast. Add bay leaf. Cover and bake at 325 degrees for approximately 2 to 2-1/2 hours, or until meat is almost tender. Add carrots, mushrooms, and celery to roast. Cover, continue to bake until meat and vegetables are tender. Discard bay leaf. If liquid is thin, thicken with flour. Serve hot.

Blue-Plate Burger Special

1 pound ground venison
1 teaspoon salt
1-1/2 teaspoons horseradish
2 teaspoons prepared mustard
1-1/2 teaspoons Worcestershire sauce
3 tablespoons ketchup
1 small onion, minced
1/2 cup soft bread crumbs
1/4 cup evaporated milk
2 tablespoons butter or margarine (optional)

Combine all ingredients in a medium-sized mixing bowl. Shape mixture into individual patties.

Method 1) To broil, lay patties on broiler pan. Broil 3 inches below source of heat, about 6 minutes on each side for large patties; 4 minutes for smaller ones; or until brown outside and medium-done inside.

Method 2) To pan fry, melt the 2 tablespoons butter in a skillet. Add patties, cook until browned on outside and no longer pink on inside. Turn patties over several times during cooking.

Braised Venison Cubes with Vegetables

2 pounds boneless venison cut in 1-1/2 inch pieces
2 tablespoons bacon drippings or vegetable oil
2 teaspoons salt
1/8 teaspoon pepper
Water
6 medium potatoes, peeled and chunked
6 medium carrots, peeled and chunked
1 large onion, chopped
1 package (9-ounce) frozen cut green beans
Flour, quick-mixing

In a Dutch oven or electric skillet, brown meat in hot bacon fat. Pour off drippings. Add salt and pepper. Add water to cover meat. Cover tightly and cook slowly for 1-1/2 hours. Add potatoes, carrots, onions, and green beans. Cover and continue cooking for an additional 30 minutes, or until meat and vegetables are tender.

Remove meat and vegetables to a heated platter or serving dish. Add enough water to cooking liquid in pan to make 2 cups. Thicken liquid with flour for gravy.

Breaded Venison Cutlets with Mushroom Sauce

1 pound venison
3/4 cup flour
1/2 teaspoon salt
1/4 teaspoon ground pepper
2 eggs
1/4 cup milk
2 cups fresh white bread crumbs, finely ground
1/4 cup butter or margarine

Cut meat into 1/2 inch thick slices. Use flat side of a meat mallet to flatten meat to 1/4 inch thickness. In a small bowl, beat eggs and milk to a foam. Combine flour, salt and pepper. Place bread crumbs in shallow bowl. Dredge meat slices in flour coating both sides. Dip slices in egg mixture and then in the bread crumbs. Coat meat completely with crumbs.

Melt butter in a heavy skillet on medium heat. Add meat slices and brown. Turn and brown other side. Cook for about 5 to 7 minutes until meat is cooked through. To serve, place two cutlets on a plate and spoon Mushroom Sauce over tops.

Mushroom Sauce

2 beef bouillon cubes
2 cups hot water
1 tablespoon butter
1/2 cup minced green onions
2-1/2 cups sliced, fresh mushrooms or substitute canned, drained mushrooms
1/2 cup white sherry
1/4 cup brandy
Flour, quick-mixing (optional)

Dissolve bouillon in the hot water. In a sauté pan, melt butter. Add minced onions and mushrooms; sauté onions until almost tender. Add sherry, brandy and dissolved bouillon; bring to a boil. Simmer for 10 to 15 minutes, reducing liquid to about half the volume. Sauce should not be thick. However, if too thin, sprinkle in a small amount of flour and stir until slightly thickened.

Note: Adjust the amount of sherry and brandy to suit your taste.

Burgundy Venison Ragout

A perfect entrée for entertaining

3 slices bacon, cut into 2-inch pieces
3 pounds venison cut into 1-inch cubes
2 cups dry red wine
1/2 cup water
1 can (14-1/2-ounce) beef broth
1/2 teaspoon thyme leaves
1 garlic clove, minced
1 bay leaf
2 medium onions, cut in chunks
20 baby carrots
2 tablespoons butter, softened
2 tablespoons all-purpose flour

Use an ovenproof Dutch oven and cook bacon until crisp. Remove bacon and set aside. Brown venison cubes in bacon drippings. Stir in wine, water, beef broth, thyme, garlic, and bay leaf. Cover and bake at 350 degrees for 2 hours. Stir occasionally. Add bacon, onions, and carrots. Continue to bake an additional 1 hour or until meat and vegetables are tender.

Remove meat and vegetables with a slotted spoon to a bowl; keep warm. Discard bay leaf. In a small bowl, combine butter and flour, Gradually add 1/2 cup cooking liquid, stirring until smooth. Add flour mixture back into pan juices. Cook over medium heat until mixture thickens, stirring constantly. Return meat and vegetables to Dutch oven and heat through. Spoon contents into a serving dish.

Cabinhaus Venison Stew

One of my family's all-time favorites

2 pounds boneless venison stew meat cut into 1/2-inch cubes
1/2 cup flour
1/2 teaspoon celery salt
1/4 teaspoon pepper
2 to 3 tablespoons bacon drippings
2 large onions, chopped
3-3/4 cups water
6 beef bouillon cubes
1/2 teaspoon Worcestershire sauce
1 garlic clove, minced
Salt and pepper
4 to 5 potatoes, peeled and cubed
3 to 4 carrots, peeled and sliced

Combine flour, celery salt, and pepper in a bowl. Dredge venison in seasoned flour. Reserve flour. In a Dutch oven or heavy kettle, melt bacon drippings. Brown on all sides. Remove meat as it browns and set aside. Add more bacon drippings if needed and brown the onions.

Add water to Dutch oven, bring to boiling and then dissolve the bouillon cubes. Add in Worcestershire sauce, garlic, meat and onions to kettle. Season with salt, or celery salt, and pepper. Cover; simmer for about 2 hours, or until meat is tender. Stir occasionally.

Add vegetables 30 minutes before the end of cooking, and continue simmering. Stew will thicken somewhat during cooking. For thicker stew, use remaining 1/4 cup reserved flour blended with cold water. Stir in flour to thicken as desired.

Variation: Follow recipe above but add peas, tomatoes, corn, or green beans. Drain liquid if using canned vegetables. Add a dash or two of Tabasco sauce to spice things up.

Cheesy Venison Loaf

1 pound ground venison
1/2 pound ground lean pork
12 salted crackers, crushed fine
1/2 cup tomato catsup
1 egg
1 medium onion, minced
1/4 teaspoon salt
Dash pepper
1 tablespoon green pepper, minced
1/8 teaspoon prepared mustard
1/4 cup celery, minced
1/8 teaspoon garlic salt
2 teaspoons Worcestershire sauce
1/2 cup grated Parmesan cheese

Lightly spray a loaf pan with vegetable spray. In a bowl, combine the first 13 ingredients, except the Parmesan cheese. Mix well. Press meat mixture into loaf pan. Sprinkle top with Parmesan cheese. Bake at 350 degrees approximately 1-3/4 hours or until center of loaf is no longer pink. If cheese is browning too fast, cover with foil.

A wire whisk works well for stirring and blending sauces and gravies.

Chunky Italian Venison Soup

1 pound ground venison
1 large onion, minced
2 tablespoons olive oil
2 cans (14-1/2-ounce) Italian tomatoes
1 can (10-3/4-ounce) tomato soup
1 can (14-1/2-ounce) beef broth
1 cup water
3 drops Kitchen Bouquet
2 garlic cloves, minced
1 tablespoon Italian seasoning
1 teaspoon dried basil
1 teaspoon dried oregano
1 teaspoon seasoned salt
1 tablespoon chili powder
1 can (16-ounce) pinto beans, drained
1 can (16-ounce) Italian green beans, drained
2 carrots, peeled and sliced
1 zucchini, chopped, or 1 can (16-ounce) zucchini, undrained
8 ounces rotini noodles, cooked
Grated Parmesan cheese

Heat olive oil in a Dutch oven and cook venison and onion. Crumble venison
into fine pieces while cooking. Drain off any cooking liquid. Discard. Stir in
tomatoes, and next 14 ingredients. Bring to a boil; reduce heat. Simmer, stirring
occasionally for 45 minutes. Stir in cooked pasta. Sprinkle each serving with
Parmesan cheese.

Country Venison Meat Loaf

2 pounds ground venison
3 white or whole-wheat bread slices
2 tablespoons salad oil
1 medium onion, chopped
1 rib celery, finely chopped
1 medium carrot, finely shredded
1-1/2 teaspoons salt
1/4 teaspoon coarse ground black pepper
1 egg
1 can (8-ounce) tomato sauce
1 tablespoon light brown sugar
1 tablespoon cider vinegar
1 tablespoon prepared mustard

Process bread slices into crumbs in a food chopper or blender. In a small skillet, heat oil over medium heat. Add onion and celery; cook 10 minutes, stirring occasionally. In a large bowl, combine onion, celery, and bread crumbs. Add in ground venison, carrot, salt, pepper, egg, and 1/2 can of tomato sauce. Stir thoroughly to mix.

In an 8- by 12-inch baking dish or 3-quart casserole, shape meat mixture into a loaf. In a small bowl, combine brown sugar, vinegar, mustard, and remaining tomato sauce. Spoon sauce over meat loaf. Bake in a 350-degree oven 1-1/2 hours or until middle of loaf is no longer pink.

Cream-Dipped Venison Steaks

1 to 1-1/2 pounds venison steaks cut about 1/2-inch thick
1/4 cup thick cream or evaporated milk
1/4 cup all-purpose flour
1 teaspoon salt
1/4 teaspoon pepper
1/8 teaspoon garlic powder
3 tablespoons butter or margarine

Pound steaks with a meat mallet. Combine flour, salt, pepper, and garlic powder. Dip steaks into cream; dredge in flour mixture. Melt butter in a hot skillet; brown meat on both sides. Serve hot.

Creamy Venison Stroganoff

1-1/2 pounds ground or cubed venison
2 tablespoons butter or vegetable oil
1/2 cup onion, minced
1/2 cup celery, chopped
1 clove garlic, minced
2 tablespoons quick-mixing flour
2 teaspoons salt
1/2 teaspoon fresh ground pepper
1/2 teaspoon paprika
1 pound fresh mushrooms, sliced
   Or 2 (8-ounce) cans sliced mushrooms, drained
1 can (10-3/4-ounce) cream-of-chicken soup
1 cup sour cream
Fresh parsley, snipped (optional)

Melt butter in a skillet over medium heat. **Hamburger:** Fry until no longer pink. Crumble while cooking. **Cubed:** Brown on all sides. Remove to a dish. Set aside.

Sauté onion and celery until soft, but not brown. Stir in garlic, flour, salt, pepper, paprika, and mushrooms. Cook mixture for 5 minutes. Add soup; blend into mixture. **Hamburger:** Add hamburger, simmer uncovered for 20 minutes. **Cubed:** Add cubes. Cover, simmering for 1 hour or until meat is tender. Stir in sour cream just before serving; sprinkle with parsley. Heat through, but do not boil. Serve immediately on rice, noodles, toast, or mashed potatoes.

Crock-Pot Venison Vegetable Soup

1 pound venison steak, cut into 1/2-inch cubes
1 can (14-1/2 ounces) diced tomatoes, undrained
3 cups water
3 medium potatoes, peeled and cubed
2 medium onions, diced
2 cups celery, sliced
2 carrots, pared and sliced
5 beef bouillon cubes
1 teaspoon Worcestershire sauce
1 teaspoon garlic powder
1 teaspoon dried basil
1 teaspoon dried oregano
1-1/2 cups frozen mixed vegetables
Salt and pepper to taste

In a Crock-Pot, combine the first 12 ingredients. Cover, cook on high for 6 hours. Add frozen mixed vegetables. Cover, continue to cook on high an additional 2 hours or until meat and vegetables are tender. Serve with a mixed green salad and crusty hard rolls.

Daybreak Venison Breakfast

1 pound ground venison
2 tablespoons vegetable oil
3 medium onions, diced
1 can (14-1/2-ounce) peas
1 can (10-3/4-ounce) cream of celery soup
Salt and pepper to taste
Buttered toast

In a skillet, brown ground venison in hot oil. Add onions and cook until tender. Drain peas; reserve liquid. To venison, add peas, soup, salt and pepper. Stir in liquid from peas to desired consistency. Cook, stirring frequently until mixture is hot. To serve, spoon mixture over buttered toast.

Deer Camp Venison Patties

Great served with scrambled eggs and a cup of hot coffee

1-1/2 pounds ground venison
1/2 pound ground fresh pork
3 tablespoons fine bread crumbs
2 tablespoons onion, finely chopped
2 teaspoons salt
1 egg, lightly beaten
1/8 teaspoon chili powder
1/4 teaspoon garlic salt
1/8 teaspoon pepper
1/2 cup butter or bacon drippings
1/3 cup water

In a medium-sized mixing bowl, blend the first 9 ingredients together thoroughly. Shape into individual patties. Melt butter in skillet and brown patties on both sides, turning frequently. Add water and cover. Simmer 15 to 20 minutes, or until center is no longer pink.

When making meatballs, dip your fingers in water before rolling. This will prevent stickiness.

Delectable Venison Pie

2 medium potatoes, peeled and quartered
1 pound ground venison
2 tablespoons olive oil
3/4 cup celery, sliced thin
3/4 cup green onions, sliced
1 large carrot, peeled and chopped fine
1 garlic clove, minced
1/2 teaspoon dried thyme
1/2 teaspooon rubbed sage
1/2 teaspoon salt
1/4 teaspoon pepper
1 teaspoon dried parsley
1/3 cup chili sauce
1 box prepared pie crusts (2 packages)
1 tablespoon mustard
1 tablespoon milk

In a saucepan, cook potatoes until tender in boiling water. Drain, mash potatoes; set aside. Heat oil in a skillet; brown venison. Drain off cooking liquid. Stir in next 10 ingredients. Add potatoes to mixture; stir to blend.

Place 1 pie crust in a 9-inch pie plate; brush with mustard. Add meat mixture. Top with remaining pie crust. Seal edges. Cut slits into top crust. Brush top crust with milk. Bake at 450 degrees for 10 minutes. Reduce heat to 350 degrees; bake 30 minutes longer or until crust is golden brown. Serve with extra chili sauce or ketchup on the side.

Easy Venison Stew

In a hurry? Save time and use the pressure cooker

2 pounds venison cut into 1-1/2 inch chunks
2 tablespoons salad oil
1/2 cup red wine
1/4 pound bacon, diced
1 can (16-ounce) stewed tomatoes, undrained
1 large onion, minced
2 carrots, peeled and sliced
1 rib celery, sliced
1/2 garlic clove, minced
1 whole bay leaf
1 teaspoon salt
1 teaspoon thyme leaves
1/2 cup water

In large bowl or plastic zip-top bag, prepare a marinade of the salad oil and wine. Add venison chunks; turn over to coat with marinade. Cover and refrigerate for 4 hours, turning meat often.

Drain meat and discard marinade. In a 4-quart pressure cooker over medium heat, fry bacon until lightly crisp. Add meat, cook until well browned. Place tomatoes, onion, carrots, and celery on top of meat. Add garlic, bay leaf, salt, thyme, and water. Cover, set control at 10 and cook for 20 minutes after control jiggles. Remove pan from heat. Reduce pressure according to manufacturer's instructions before uncovering. Discard bay leaf. Serve over noodles.

Note: Can be prepared in a Crock-Pot. Follow recipe above. Place in Crock-Pot; set on low and cook for 8 hours, or on high for 6 hours, or until meat is tender.

Don't cook with a wine you wouldn't also drink.

Flavorful Grilled Venison Steaks

2 to 2-1/2 pounds venison cut into 3/4- to 1-inch size steaks
Bacon slices
Grill seasoning (prepared mix)
Worcestershire sauce

Lightly spray grill rack with non-stick cooking spray. Heat grill to medium-high heat. Rub a small amount of Worcestershire sauce over both sides of steak. Season steaks with prepared grill seasoning on both sides. Wrap 1 or 2 bacon slices around outside edge of each steak. Secure bacon with toothpicks to hold in place. Place steaks on grill rack. Sear meat on both sides. Continue to grill until meat is cooked according to your tastes.

Fricasseed Venison Liver

1 pound venison liver
1/2 teaspoon salt
1/8 teaspoon pepper
1/4 cup bacon fat
1/4 cup all-purpose flour
1/2 teaspoon poultry seasoning
1/2 teaspoon celery salt
1 cup canned tomatoes, undrained
3 medium green peppers, seeded and chopped
1 cup white onions, chopped
1-1/2 cups water
Cooked noodles

Cut liver into thin slices. Wash liver, drain, and place in a bowl. Cover liver with boiling water. Let stand 5 minutes. Drain and wipe dry.

Combine the flour, salt and pepper in a shallow bowl. Dredge liver pieces in mixture. Brown liver quickly in hot bacon drippings. Add all vegetables and water. Add celery salt and poultry seasoning. Cover, simmer 45 minutes. Serve with cooked, buttered noodles.

Grandma Florence's Sauerbraten

Team up with German potato pancakes and German-style red cabbage

3 to 3-1/2 pounds venison roast
2 onions, sliced
2 whole bay leaves
12 peppercorns
1/8 teaspoon ground cumin
6 whole cloves
1-1/2 teaspoons salt
1-1/2 cups red wine vinegar
1 cup boiling water
3 tablespoons vegetable oil
12 gingersnaps, crushed (3/4 cup)
2 teaspoons sugar

Place venison in a glass baking dish or large heavy plastic zip-top bag. Add in onions, bay leaves, peppercorns, cloves, cumin, salt, vinegar, and boiling water. Cover dish tightly with plastic wrap; refrigerate at least 3 days, turning meat twice a day with tongs. Never pierce meat when turning.

Drain meat, reserving marinade. Heat oil in skillet over medium-high heat. Brown meat on all sides. Add marinade. Cover, reduce heat, and simmer 3 to 3-1/2 hours or until meat is tender. Remove roast; slice into serving portions. Place meat and onions into a casserole dish; cover, and keep warm.

Strain and measure liquid from skillet. If needed, add water to measure 2-1/2 cups of liquid. Pour liquid into skillet. Cover and simmer for 10 minutes. Stir crushed gingersnaps and sugar into liquid. Cover and simmer gently an additional 3 minutes. Serve gravy with roast.

Grilled Marinated Venison Chops

1-1/2 pounds venison chops or steaks cut 1/2-inch thick
1/3 cup red wine vinegar
1/3 cup ketchup
1 tablespoon Worcestershire sauce
1/4 teaspoon salt
1 teaspoon dry mustard
1/8 teaspoon pepper
2 cloves garlic, finely minced

Place chops or steaks in a shallow bowl or plastic zip-top bag. Combine remaining ingredients in a bowl; pour over chops. If using a bowl, cover with plastic wrap. Refrigerate for 3 hours, turning chops occasionally.

Preheat grill to medium-high heat. Drain off marinade, and reserve for basting. Place chops in a wire grill basket or lay directly on grates. Baste with marinade until chops are cooked according to personal taste. Season with salt and pepper if desired.

Heart of Venison with Vegetables

1 venison heart
Water
1 tablespoon salt
4 tablespoons all-purpose flour
1 teaspoon salt
1/4 teaspoon pepper
4 tablespoons bacon drippings
2 cup carrots, peeled and diced
1-1/2 cups celery, diced
1 medium onion, sliced
2 medium potatoes, peeled and cubed
2 tablespoons dried parsley

Clean and wash out heart in cold water. In a bowl, cover heart with cold water and 1 tablespoon salt. Soak in salt water overnight or all day. Rinse, drain, and wipe dry.

Slice heart crosswise in 1/2 inch slices. Remove the tough white membrane. Mix flour, salt and pepper in a bowl; dredge heart slices in mixture. Melt bacon drippings in a heavy skillet, and sauté slices until lightly browned. Add just enough water to cover meat. Cover, reduce heat and simmer for 1 hour. Add more water or salt and pepper, if necessary. Add in vegetables, cover and continue to simmer until meat and vegetables are tender.

Hearty Venison Stew

3 pounds venison cut into bite-size pieces
1/2 cup all-purpose flour
3 tablespoons vegetable oil or bacon drippings
1-1/2 cups hot water
1 cup red wine
1 teaspoon dried thyme
1 teaspoon dried marjoram
1 teaspoon dried basil
1 teaspoon dried parsley
1 large onion, sliced
1-1/2 teaspoons salt
1/2 teaspoon coarse black pepper
4 carrots, peeled and quartered
3 potatoes, peeled and chunked
2 ribs celery, cut in pieces

Place flour in a plastic zip-top bag. Coat meat in flour; shake off excess. Heat vegetable oil in a Dutch oven or deep kettle; brown the meat. Add hot water, wine, herbs, onions, salt, and pepper. Cover and bring to a boil. Lower heat and simmer for 2 hours. Add vegetables; cover, and continue to simmer until meat and vegetables are tender. Serve hot.

Hearty Venison Stroganoff

A zesty twist to a favorite dish

1-1/2 pounds venison cut into 1/2-inch cubes
1 recipe 1-2-3 Meat Marinade (see p. 239)
1/2 cup all-purpose flour
3 tablespoons olive oil
1 medium onion, chopped
1 garlic clove, minced
1 can (8-ounce) mushrooms, drained, reserve 1/2 of liquid
1/2 teaspoon hot sauce
1 can (10-3/4-ounce) tomato soup
1 tablespoon Worcestershire sauce
1/4 teaspoon salt
1-1/2 cups sour cream

Prepare 1-2-3 Meat Marinade in a bowl; put in venison cubes. Marinate for 20 minutes, turning cubes occasionally. Remove venison from marinade.

Place flour in a bowl; dredge venison. Heat oil in large skillet over medium-high heat. Brown meat on all sides. Add onions, garlic and mushrooms, mushroom liquid, soup, hot sauce, and Worcestershire sauce. Salt to taste. Cover and simmer for 1 hour; stir occasionally. Stir in sour cream just before serving. Heat through, but do not boil. Serve over hot rice or buttered noodles.

Herbed Breakfast Sausage

1 pound ground venison
1/2 pound ground pork
1/4 teaspoon marjoram
1/4 teaspoon oregano
1/8 teaspoon black pepper
1/8 teaspoon sage
1/8 teaspoon thyme
1/8 teaspoon salt
1/4 teaspoon garlic powder

In a large mixing bowl, combine venison and pork. Add all seasonings to meat mixture. Mix well to distribute seasonings evenly throughout the meat. Press equal amounts of mixture into patties. Fry in a skillet at low heat until no longer pink in the middle.

Note: To freeze, lay individual patties in single layer on cookie sheet. Place in freezer. Remove when completely frozen. Package in freezer wrap or containers in meal-size portions.

Italian Venison on a Bun

Experience a tangy taste sensation with these hot, meaty sandwiches

4 to 6 pounds venison roast
3 beef bouillon cubes
2-1/2 to 3 cups water
1 green pepper, chopped
1 large onion, chopped
1 teaspoon dried marjoram
1 teaspoon dried thyme
1 teaspoon dried oregano
1 teaspoon dried sweet basil
1 teaspoon Worcestershire sauce
1/2 teaspoon liquid hot pepper sauce (add more if your taste buds desire)
Garlic salt

Roast venison meat at 325 degrees for 2 to 2-1/2 hours, or until meat thermometer registers medium rare. Remove roast from pan and cool completely. Save pan juices. When meat has cooled, slice it thin.

In a saucepan, add the pan drippings, bouillon cubes, water, green pepper, onion, and remaining seasonings. Bring to a simmer; simmer for 15 minutes. Remove from heat. Add sliced venison, and marinate overnight in refrigerator. Serve hot or cold on buns, hard rolls, or French bread.

Italian Venison Stew

2 pounds venison, cubed
1/4 cup butter
3 tablespoons olive oil
2 cups celery, sliced
1 large onion, chopped
1 green pepper, seeded and chopped
1 can (16 to 20-ounce) Italian style diced tomatoes, drained
2 large potatoes, peeled and diced
1-1/2 cups canned beef broth
3 tablespoons brown sugar
1/2 teaspoon dried Italian seasoning
1 tablespoon vinegar
1 tablespoon dried parsley

Melt butter in a Dutch oven or large kettle; add oil and heat. Brown venison cubes on all sides. Add remaining ingredients. Cover; simmer for 1-1/2 to 2 hours or until meat is tender.

Note: Prepare in Crock-Pot. Brown meat in a skillet. Follow remainder of recipe.

Kentucky Hill Country Venison Roast

2 pounds venison roast
1/2 cup beef broth
1 package dry onion soup mix
Worcestershire sauce to taste
1 pound package maple-flavored bacon
Salt and pepper
1 large onion, sliced
1 pound fresh mushrooms, sliced

Place roast in a baking pan. Add beef broth. Sprinkle soup mix over roast; salt and pepper as desired. Lay one-half of the bacon strips on top of roast. Cover pan; bake at 225 degrees for 3 to 3-1/2 hours until tender.

Remove bacon from roast. In a skillet, fry bacon from roast with uncooked bacon, until crisp. Remove bacon and crumble into pieces. Fry sliced onions and mushrooms in bacon drippings until just tender. Return bacon pieces back into onions and mushrooms. Stir to combine flavors.

Remove roast from pan and slice. Return sliced pieces back to baking pan. Pour skillet ingredients over sliced meat. Cover, place baking pan back into a 225-degree oven for about 1/2 hour to absorb the juices.

Marinated Braised Venison

Marinade:

1/4 cup olive oil
1 cup dry red wine
1 clove garlic, minced
2 tablespoons brandy
1 whole bay leaf
Few sprigs parsley or 1/4 teaspoon dried parsley

Mix ingredients together.

3 pounds sliced venison shoulder or flank meat
1/2 to 3/4 pounds bacon
1 tablespoon quick-mixing flour

Prepare enough marinade to cover meat. Refrigerate overnight. Next day, fry bacon in a skillet until crisp. Drain, and set aside. Drain marinated meat and pat dry with paper toweling. Reserve marinade. Discard bay leaf. Braise meat in bacon drippings on all sides. Place in a baking dish. Have skillet on low heat. Stir flour into skillet and cook for 2 minutes. Stir in reserved marinade; pour over meat.

Bake in a 350-degree oven for 1-1/2 hours or until meat is tender. Remove to a warm platter. Garnish with reserved crumbled bacon sprinkled over meat.

Marinated Venison Cutlets with Cream Sauce

12 venison cutlets, about 3/8-inch thick
Red Wine Marinade (see p. 251)
1/2 teaspoon salt
Pepper
Flour, all-purpose
2 tablespoons butter or margarine
1 tablespoon vegetable oil
1 cup heavy cream
2 tablespoons red currant jelly
1/2 teaspoon fresh lemon juice

Prepare either marinade mixture. Add cutlets and marinate for 4 hours in refrigerator. Remove cutlets and strain marinade. Save marinade. Pat cutlets dry with paper towel. Sprinkle with salt and pepper. Dip cutlets in flour; shake off excess.

In a heavy skillet, add butter and oil. Heat over medium-high heat. Fry cutlets for 2 minutes on each side or until well browned. Remove cutlets; set aside. Pour off all but a thin film of frying agent from skillet.

Carefully pour 3/4 cup of the marinade through a strainer into the skillet. Bring marinade to a gentle boil while scraping bottom of pan to loosen all browned particles. Reduce heat to simmer cooking until liquid is reduced to half its volume.

Return cutlets to skillet. Simmer for 5 minutes, basting cutlets several times. Remove cutlets to heated serving platter. To the skillet add cream, currant jelly and lemon juice. Use a whisk to blend mixture. Simmer until jelly dissolves, whisking constantly. Pour cream sauce over cutlets and serve.

Marinated Venison Kabobs

4 tablespoons vegetable oil
2 tablespoons maple syrup
2 teaspoons soy sauce
2 tablespoons lemon juice
1/2 teaspoon garlic powder
1/2 teaspoon onion salt
1-1/2 to 2 pounds venison, cut into 2-inch chunks
Water, as needed
Whole mushrooms
Large onion chunks
Green, red, or yellow pepper chunks

Combine first 7 ingredients in a ceramic bowl or plastic zip-top bag. Mix well. Add venison chunks to marinade. If needed, add water to marinade to cover meat. Refrigerate and marinate for 1 hour. Remove meat; discard marinade.

Place mushrooms, onions, and peppers in a large bowl. Cover with boiling water. Keep vegetables in water for 10 minutes. This helps vegetables from drying out when grilling. Drain. Assemble venison and vegetables on skewers. Cook over a medium hot grill until meat is cooked until desired doneness.

Marinated Venison Loin Medallions

2 pounds venison loin, cleaned and trimmed
1 cup balsamic vinegar
1/4 cup olive oil
1 garlic clove, crushed
1 teaspoon fresh ground black pepper
2 tablespoons butter
3 slices bacon (optional)

Combine vinegar, oil, garlic, and pepper in a bowl or plastic zip-top bag. Add loin to mixture. Marinate for 1 to 2 hours. Remove loin.

Method 1) To prepare for baking, melt butter in a hot skillet. Brown all sides of loin. Place the loin in a roasting pan. Lay slices of bacon on top of loin. Roast at 325 degrees for 30 to 60 minutes, or until desired-degree of doneness. Slice into 1/2-inch medallions

Method 2) To grill, have grill at medium-high heat. Sear loin on all sides to seal in juices. Grill until desired doneness. Slice and serve hot.

Mostaccioli Venison Stew

A very nutritious meal

1-1/2 pounds venison, cut into 1-inch cubes
2 tablespoons oil
1-1/2 teaspoons salt
1 teaspoon paprika
1/2 teaspoon chili powder
2-1/2 cups water
1 can (16-ounce) whole tomatoes, cut up
1 cup carrots, sliced
1/2 cup celery, sliced
1/2 package frozen green beans
1 small clove garlic, minced
1 medium onion, sliced
1 cup uncooked mostaccioli

In a Dutch oven or large kettle, brown venison cubes in hot oil. Add remaining ingredients except mostaccioli; mix well. Cover and simmer for 2 hours or until meat is tender. Stir in mostaccioli and cook 12 to 15 minutes or until tender. Serve hot.

Cut meat into steaks, cubes, or thin slices while it is still partially frozen.

Mushroom Venison Ragu

1 pound ground venison
2 tablespoons butter
2-1/2 cups heavy cream
1/2 teaspoon salt
1/8 teaspoon nutmeg
4 tablespoons butter or margarine
1/4 cup green onions, minced
2 large cloves garlic, minced
1 pound fresh mushrooms, sliced
1 cup freshly grated Parmigiano-Reggiano cheese
1/2 teaspoon freshly ground black pepper
1 pound refrigerated cheese tortellini

In a skillet, melt 2 tablespoons butter; add ground venison. Cook until meat is no longer pink. Remove meat with a slotted spoon. Set meat aside.

In medium saucepan, combine cream, salt and nutmeg. Bring to boil; reduce heat. Cook uncovered about 15 minutes, or until cream has reduced by one-fourth and thickened.

Melt butter in a large skillet over medium heat. Add green onions and garlic; sauté about 4 minutes. Increase heat to medium-high; add mushrooms. Cover, cook until mushrooms begin to render their juices. Uncover, cook over high heat until all juices have evaporated. Add cooked venison. Reduce heat to medium. Stir in cream, 1/3 cup of the grated cheese, and pepper. Cover and keep warm.

Cook tortellini in large pot of boiling salted water until tender. Drain; return tortellini to pot. Add venison mushroom sauce to tortellini and toss well. Serve with additional grated cheese.

Mustard Loin Medallions

1/2 cup seasoned dry bread crumbs
1/2 teaspoon dried thyme
1/4 teaspoon garlic powder
1/4 teaspoon onion powder
1-1/2 pounds venison loin
1/4 cup Dijon mustard
1 tablespoon butter or margarine, melted

Combine bread crumbs, thyme, garlic and onion powder in a shallow container. Cut loin into slices. Flatten slices with meat mallet to 1/4-inch thickness. Combine mustard and butter; brush on each side of loin, then coat with bread crumb mixture. Place in a greased shallow baking pan. Bake, uncovered, at 425 degrees for 15 to 20 minutes, or until loins are tender. Turn once during baking.

No Peek Venison Stew

2-1/2 pounds venison, cut into 1-inch cubes
3 large carrots, peeled, cut into chunks
3 large potatoes, peeled, cut into 1-inch cubes
2 large onions, chopped
3 cloves garlic, minced
1 teaspoon celery salt
1 teaspoon dried thyme
2 teaspoons pepper
2-1/2 cups tomato juice
1/2 cup dry red wine
1 tablespoon Dijon mustard
2 tablespoons light brown sugar
3-1/2 tablespoons tapioca

Place all ingredients in a Dutch oven or large casserole dish. Mix to blend ingredients. Cover and bake at 275 degrees for approximately 5 hours, without peeking or disturbing.

Variation: Use a Crock-Pot or slow-cooker and set temperature on low. To prepare stew, reduce the amount of tomato juice to 2 cups and the wine to 1/4 cup. Cook for up to 8 hours.

Old-Fashioned Venison Liver and Bacon

1 pound liver, sliced thin
12 slices bacon
Salt and pepper
1 medium onion, sliced

Rinse liver in water. Drain. Place in a bowl and cover liver with boiling water. Let stand for 5 minutes. Drain. Wipe liver dry.

Brown bacon in a hot frying pan until crisp. Remove; set aside. Salt and pepper liver, then lay in pan. Over medium heat, fry liver about 10 minutes or until brown. Turn frequently. Remove when cooked to a warm dish. Keep warm. Add more bacon drippings to skillet; brown onions until tender. To serve, crumble bacon pieces over top and spread onions around liver.

Oriental Venison Pepper Steak

Serve over rice or pasta

2 tablespoons oil
1 to 1-1/2 pounds venison steak cut in strips
2 tablespoons minced onion
1 clove garlic, minced
1 green pepper seeded and diced
1 red or yellow pepper seeded and diced
1 cup beef consommé
1 cup Roma tomatoes, diced
1-1/2 tablespoons cornstarch
2 teaspoons Teriyaki sauce
1/4 cup cold water

Heat oil in a large skillet over high heat; add meat. Add onion and garlic; sauté until brown. Add diced peppers and beef consommé. Cover, simmer for about 30 minutes or until meat is tender. Add diced tomatoes and simmer an additional 5 minutes.

Blend cornstarch, soy sauce, and water in a small bowl. Blend into pan liquid. Heat to boiling, stirring constantly. Continue stirring until mixture has thickened and is translucent. Serve over fluffy rice or hot noodles.

Piquant Venison Roast

1 venison roast
1/4 pound bacon cut into pieces
1 package dry onion soup mix
1 can (10-3/4-ounce) cream of mushroom soup
3 cloves garlic, minced
1-1/2 tablespoons honey
1 tablespoon prepared mustard
1/2 cup red wine
3 tablespoons olive oil
Juice of 1/2 lime

Place roast in small roaster or large casserole dish. Make several slits in roast; insert bacon pieces into the slits.

In a bowl, combine soup mix, soup and the next six ingredients. Mix well. Pour mixture over roast. Cover meat with four or five strips of bacon. Cover tightly with foil.

Bake at 325 degrees for 2 to 3 hours, depending on size of roast, Baste several times with pan juices. Do not overcook meat. When roast is tender, slice thinly, and serve with pan juices.

Make stews and soups a day ahead. The flavors will develop and become stronger.

Pot Roast of Venison

Haunch or loin of venison
3 medium-sized onions, chopped
4 carrots, peeled and sliced
2 small turnips, peeled and diced
4 ribs celery, sliced
1/4 teaspoon dried parsley
1/8 teaspoon dried rosemary
1/8 teaspoon dried thyme
2 whole bay leaves
2 strips lemon peel
Salt
8 peppercorns
1 cup dry red wine
1 cup water
1/2 cup sour cream

Place all vegetables and herbs in a Dutch oven with red wine and water. Bring to a boil. Reduce heat, cover and simmer for 30 minutes. Season with salt to taste. Add venison and cover. Simmer for 2 hours.

Remove meat; place in a roasting pan. Strain liquid from Dutch oven and blend in 1/2 cup of sour cream. Pour mixture over meat. Cover and bake at 300 degrees until meat is tender, about 1 to 1-1/2 hours.

Quick-Cooked Venison Roast

For those days when time is short, use a pressure cooker

4 or 5 pound venison chuck roast
1/4 teaspoon salt
1/2 teaspoon celery salt
1 tablespoon poultry seasoning
1/4 teaspoon black pepper
3 or 4 tablespoons bacon drippings
2 onions, chopped
2 whole bay leaves
2 cups hot water
2 tablespoons quick-mixing flour
1 tablespoon cold water

In a small bowl, combine salt, celery salt, poultry seasoning and black pepper. Rub roast with this mixture. Melt bacon drippings in pressure cooker and then brown roast on all sides. Add onions, bay leaves, and hot water. Put on pressure cover, set control at 10 pounds of pressure. Cook for 50 to 60 minutes after control jiggles. Reduce pressure as manufacturer directs. Remove meat and place in a warm serving dish. Discard bay leaves. To make gravy, add enough water to pan juices to make 1 cup. Blend flour and water; stir into liquid. Continue cooking and stirring until desired consistency. Serve with dumplings.

Note: Follow manufacturer's instructions for pressure cooking.

Roast Venison with Sherry Sauce

2 to 5 pounds venison roast
2 tablespoons soft butter
Salt and pepper
2 to 3 onions, sliced thin
1 whole bay leaf
1/2 teaspoon dried parsley
1/2 teaspoon dried thyme
1/4 cup water
1/2 cup sherry
1/8 teaspoon ground cloves
1 cup beef broth

Spread butter over top of roast and season with salt and pepper. Arrange meat in a roasting pan with onions, bay leaf, parsley, thyme, and water. Cover and roast in a 350-degree oven, approximately 1 to 1-1/2 hours or until meat is tender. Remove roast from the pan. Wrap roast in aluminum foil and keep in warm oven until sauce is made.

Pour pan liquid into a saucepan. Add sherry, ground cloves, and beef broth. Simmer until liquid is reduced to almost half its volume. Strain liquid and pour into serving bowl. Cut venison into serving-sized slices; arrange on a warm platter. Spoon sauce over slices and serve.

Rosemary Burgundy Venison

3 pounds venison chuck roast, cut into 1-inch cubes
1/2 pound bacon, diced
1 large onion, chopped
Salt and pepper to taste
3 tablespoons all-purpose flour
3 cups Burgundy wine
3 cups beef broth
2 tablespoons tomato paste
1 tablespoon fresh rosemary, chopped
1/2 pound fresh mushrooms, sliced
 4 carrots, peeled, sliced thin
1 tablespoon butter or margarine
1 tablespoon red currant jelly

In Dutch oven, sauté bacon until crisp. Remove bacon; set aside. Pour off all but 2 tablespoons of drippings. Sauté venison until browned on all sides. Add onions; sprinkle with salt, pepper, and flour. Cook over high heat, stirring constantly for 5 minutes. Add wine, broth, tomato paste, and rosemary. Bring to a boil. Remove Dutch oven from stovetop. Cover; place in oven. Bake in a 350-degree oven, 1-1/2 hours. During the last 1/2 hour, sauté mushrooms in butter in a skillet. Add carrots and cook for 5 minutes. Add vegetables to pan in oven; continue to cook an additional 30 minutes or until meat is tender. Transfer Dutch oven to stove burner. Stir in currant jelly before serving.

Saucy Barbecued Venison Ribs

Finger-licking good eating

Venison ribs
Water
Salt and pepper
Sauce:
1/2 cup tomato ketchup
1/2 cup water
1 large onion, chopped fine
1/2 cup celery, minced
1/4 cup packed brown sugar
1 teaspoon dry mustard
1/4 cup vinegar
2 tablespoons Worcestershire sauce
1/2 teaspoon soy sauce
1/2 teaspoon pepper
Dash of Tabasco sauce

Clean ribs of as much tallow as possible. Cut ribs in half and then into serving pieces. Place in a large kettle with enough water to cover. Add salt and pepper. Cover, bring to a boil. Reduce heat to simmer and cook for 1-1/2 hours. Remove ribs and place in a roasting pan. Discard water.

Mix all sauce ingredients in a bowl. Brush sauce over ribs. Cover, bake at 325 degrees until ribs are tender, about 45 minutes to 1 hour. Baste occasionally with any remaining sauce.

Note: Increase sauce recipe if needed.

Sauerkraut Venison Goulash

2 pounds venison steak, cut into 1 inch cubes
2 tablespoons vegetable oil
1 medium onion, chopped
1 teaspoon salt
1 teaspoon paprika
1/4 teaspoon pepper
1/2 teaspoon marjoram
1 cup canned diced tomatoes
1 cup carrots, sliced thin
1 can (29-ounce) sauerkraut, rinsed and drained
3/4 cup white wine
1 cup sour cream

Heat oil in large skillet; brown cubed meat. When browned, remove with a slotted spoon to a bowl. Add onion to skillet drippings, sauté 5 minutes. Return meat to skillet. Add salt, paprika, pepper, marjoram, and tomatoes. Cover, simmer until meat is tender, about 45 minutes. Add in carrots, sauerkraut, and wine. Simmer an additional 20 minutes. Stir in sour cream just before serving.

Savory Bear Roast

1 bear loin roast
1 package dry onion soup mix
1 can (10-3/4-ounce) cream of mushroom soup
Pepper
Garlic salt
1 whole bay leaf
1/8 teaspoon Worcestershire sauce
1/4 cup water

Place roast in roasting pan. Season with pepper and garlic salt. Combine dry onion soup and cream of mushroom soup. Mix to blend. Spread over top of roast. Sprinkle Worcestershire sauce over roast. Add 1/4 cup water to bottom of pan. Cover. Bake at 325 degrees about 2-1/2 to 3 hours or until meat is tender. Roasting takes approximately 35 to 45 minutes per pound of meat.

Remove roast to a casserole dish; slice and keep warm. Discard bay leaf. Make gravy with pan drippings. Pour gravy over roast and serve.

Sesame Ginger Venison Stir-Fry

3 tablespoons soy sauce
1/4 teaspoon sugar
1/4 teaspoon ground ginger
1 tablespoon peanut oil
1 pound venison steak, cut into thin strips
1 garlic clove, minced
1/2 cup beef broth
1-1/2 teaspoons cornstarch
1 to 2 tablespoons toasted sesame seeds (optional)

Combine soy sauce, sugar, and ginger in a small bowl. Heat oil in a large skillet or wok over medium-high heat. Add venison strips and garlic; stir-fry until venison is cooked through. Reduce heat to medium; stir in soy sauce mixture. In the same bowl, blend water and cornstarch until smooth; add to skillet. Bring to a boil; stir constantly until mixture becomes translucent, about 2 minutes. Sprinkle sesame seeds over meat mixture. Remove; serve over hot cooked rice or Chinese noodles.

Shredded Venison Sandwich Meat

3 to 4 pounds venison roast
1 tablespoon salt
1 tablespoon pepper
1 tablespoon garlic powder
1 tablespoon Worcestershire sauce
1 tablespoon Grey Poupon mustard
1/2 cup water

Combine salt, pepper, garlic powder, Worcestershire sauce, and mustard in a small bowl. Make a paste from this mixture; rub over roast. Place roast in a Crock-Pot. Add water. Set temperature on low; cook for 8 hours. Meat should be fork tender. Shred cooked meat with a fork. Serve hot on hamburger buns, Kaiser rolls, hard rolls, or French bread.

Rita Carlson, Nekoosa, WI

Slow Cooker Chop Suey

Serve with hot fluffy white or brown rice, or Chinese noodles

1 to 1-1/2 pounds venison cut in bite-size cubes
Flour, all-purpose
3 to 4 tablespoons vegetable oil
1 large onion, chopped fine
3 large ribs of celery, cut in chunks
3 tablespoons dark molasses
9 tablespoons soy sauce
1/4 to 1/2 cup water, if needed
1 to 2 cans (4-ounce) mushrooms, drained
1 can (14-1/2-ounce) bean sprouts, drained
1 can (14-1/2-ounce) Chinese vegetables, drained

Place flour in a plastic zip-top bag. Add cubes of meat; shake to coat with flour. Heat oil in skillet; brown the meat. As meat browns, remove and put in slow cooker. Set temperature to low. Add onions, celery, molasses, soy sauce, and water to slow cooker. Cook all day until meat is tender. Before serving, add remaining ingredients and heat thoroughly.

Sally Willman, Three Lakes, WI

Satisfying Wild Game Chili

1 pound ground venison
1 pound sausage
2 tablespoon olive oil
1 large onion, chopped
2 cans (28-ounce) stewed tomatoes
1/4 cup green chilies, chopped
2 cloves garlic, minced
1 can (15-ounce) kidney beans, undrained
1 can (16-ounce) chili beans, undrained
2 tablespoons cumin
1 tablespoon oregano
1/2 teaspoon salt
2 tablespoons chili powder
1 tablespoon ground coriander
1 cup ketchup
Shredded cheddar cheese

Brown venison and sausage in a large skillet. Remove browned meat with a slotted spoon to a large kettle. Discard remaining grease and wipe skillet with paper toweling. Heat olive oil in skillet; sauté onion, green pepper, and garlic until tender. Add to kettle with meat. Place remaining ingredients, except cheddar cheese, in kettle; bring to a boil. Reduce heat to a simmer and cook for 1 hour. Serve steaming bowls of chili topped with shredded cheddar cheese.

Note: Prepare day before to let the flavors develop.

Spicy, Oven-Barbecued Venison

1/3 cup vinegar
1/2 cup tomato ketchup
1/4 cup beef broth
2 tablespoons light brown sugar
1 tablespoon Worcestershire sauce
1 tablespoon lemon juice
Salt to taste
1/4 teaspoon freshly ground black pepper
1 clove garlic, crushed
1/4 teaspoon Tabasco sauce
1-1/2 pounds venison cut into 1-inch cubes
1/2 cup bacon drippings or vegetable oil
1 large onion, sliced
1/2 cup half and half

To prepare barbecue sauce, combine first ten ingredients in a saucepan. Bring to a boil, lower heat, and then simmer for 15 minutes. Set aside.

Using a heavy skillet, brown venison cubes in bacon drippings or oil. Transfer meat to a casserole dish or Dutch oven. Add onion slices and 1/2 of the barbecue sauce to the casserole. Bake at 350 degrees until meat is tender, about 1 hour. Add remainder of barbecue sauce as dish becomes dry. Transfer venison to a warm serving platter. In a saucepan, add half and half and pan liquid, stirring frequently until mixture comes to a boil. Remove immediately from heat and pour sauce over meat.

Spicy Venison Meatballs

Freeze a batch for quick meal preparation

3 eggs, beaten
3/4 cup milk
2 cups soft bread crumbs
1 medium onion, minced fine
1/2 cup Parmesan cheese, grated
1 teaspoon salt
1/4 teaspoon pepper
2 pounds ground venison
1 pound spicy Italian sausage
1 jar prepared brown gravy (optional)

In large bowl, combine eggs, milk, bread crumbs, onion, cheese, salt, and pepper. Mix in venison and sausage. Shape into 1 to 1-1/2-inch size balls. Bake in a shallow pan at 375 degrees for 30 to 35 minutes, or until center of meatball is no longer pink. Remove and drain. Serve as is, with brown gravy, or with spaghetti and sauce.

Note: Prepare recipe. Cook meatballs; remove, cool and freeze. Before serving, thaw, reheat in oven or add to spaghetti or favorite recipe to serve.

Spicy Venison Stew

A little out of the ordinary and oh so delicious!

1 pound venison stew meat cut into 1/2-inch cubes
1 teaspoon salt
1 teaspoon coarse ground pepper
1 teaspoon cumin
1/2 teaspoon oregano
2 tablespoons olive oil
1 onion, diced
1 red bell pepper, diced
2 cloves garlic, minced
1-1/2 cups beef broth
1/2 cup dried apricots diced, or diced mixed fruit
1/2 cup chili sauce
1 can (14-1/2-ounce) hominy or "pozole"
2 cups cooked black beans (canned beans must be rinsed)

Mix salt, pepper, cumin and oregano in a bowl. Toss venison cubes in the mixture. Heat olive oil in a skillet and brown meat in hot oil. Remove browned pieces and place in a Crock-Pot.*

Sauté onion, red pepper, and garlic, and then add to Crock-Pot. Add in beef consommé, dried apricots and chili sauce. Let mixture cook in Crock-Pot 8 to 10 hours set on low. At the end of the cooking time, add in the hominy and black beans and heat through thoroughly.

*Recipe can also be baked in the oven at 325 degrees for about 3 hours, until meat is tender.

Compliments of Clearwater Lake Distillery

Stuffed Heart of Venison

Delicious!!!

1 venison heart
2 cups salt
Cold water
Stuffing mix
1/2 cup water
1/2 cup brandy
2 tablespoons butter, melted
Salt and pepper

Clean and wash out heart in cold water. In a bowl, cover heart with cold water, add 2 cups salt. Soak in salt water overnight or all day. Rinse and drain heart for a few minutes. Wipe dry as best you can.

Prepare half of your favorite stuffing recipe. Stuff heart and close up with skewers as tightly as possible. Place any leftover stuffing in a separate dish and bake along with heart. Put heart in roasting pan. Pour 1/2 cup water, 1/2 cup brandy, and melted butter over heart. Bake, covered, in a 350-degree oven for 1-1/2 to 2 hours or until tender. Baste heart with pan juices. If more pan liquid is needed, combine equal amounts of water and brandy for basting. When tender, remove from oven. Slice and arrange on a heated platter. Pour juices over slices. Serve hot.

Stuffed Venison Birds

2 pounds venison steak, sliced
2 cups soft bread crumbs
6 tablespoons butter
1/2 cup green onions, thinly sliced
2 tablespoons parsley, chopped
4 egg yolks, beaten
3 tablespoons baked ham, chopped fine
3 tablespoons Parmesan cheese, freshly grated
1/4 teaspoon thyme
Salt and pepper to taste
2 tablespoons butter, melted

Flatten venison slices with a meat mallet or edge of a saucer to 1/4 inch thickness. In small skillet, brown bread crumbs in 4 tablespoons melted butter. In a larger skillet, melt 2 tablespoons butter; sauté onion until tender. Add parsley, egg yolks, ham, cheese, thyme, salt, and pepper. Stir to mix stuffing.

Place 1 tablespoon stuffing on each slice of venison; roll to enclose. Secure with toothpicks or string. Melt butter; dip venison rolls in butter, then in bread crumbs to coat. Lay in a shallow baking dish. Bake at 375 degrees 30 minutes, or until tender.

Sunday Venison Pot Roast

An electric skillet works great!

2 pounds venison round steak, cut 3/4 to 1-inch thick
3 tablespoons all-purpose flour
3 tablespoons vegetable oil
1/2 teaspoon salt
1 package dry onion soup mix
1 cup water
3 ribs celery, cut in 2-inch pieces
5 medium carrots, peeled and sliced
5 medium potatoes, peeled and chunked
2 tablespoons quick-mixing flour
3 tablespoons cold water

Dredge meat in flour. In a skillet, brown meat in hot vegetable oil. In a small bowl, combine salt, onion soup mix, and water; add to meat. Cover tightly, cook slowly over medium to medium-low heat for about 2 hours. If using an electric skillet, set dial temperature to 325 degrees. Add vegetables to meat. Continue cooking for an additional 45 minutes or until meat is tender and vegetables are cooked. Remove meat and vegetables with a slotted spoon, to a warm casserole dish.

In a small bowl, blend flour and cold water. Blend into cooking liquid in skillet. Heat to boiling, stirring constantly. Cook, stirring constantly, until thickened. Serve over meat and vegetables.

Tangy Venison Stroganoff

1 pound venison steak
1/4 cup butter or margarine
1/2 pound fresh mushrooms, sliced
1 cup onion, chopped
1 garlic clove, minced
2 tablespoons all-purpose flour
1 cup water
1 tablespoon lemon juice
1 tablespoon red wine vinegar
2 teaspoons beef bouillon granules
1 teaspoon dried parsley
1/2 teaspoon paprika
1/2 teaspoon salt
1/4 teaspoon pepper
1 cup sour cream

Cut venison into thin strips. Melt butter in a large skillet, over medium-high heat. Cook venison strips until no longer pink. Remove with a slotted spoon to a dish; keep warm. Add mushrooms, onion, and garlic to the skillet; cook until tender. Stir in flour; blend into ingredients. Add water, lemon juice, vinegar, bouillon, parsley, paprika, salt, pepper, and meat. Bring to a boil. Cook and stir for 3 to 5 minutes. Reduce heat to simmer. Stir in sour cream; heat through but do not boil. Serve over hot noodles.

Tender Bear Steak

1-1/2 pounds bear steak
1-1/2 tablespoon olive oil or vegetable oil
2 large onions, thinly sliced
1 can (8-ounce) sliced mushrooms, reserve 1/2 of liquid
1 can (10-3/4-ounce) cream of mushroom soup
1/4 teaspoon dried thyme
1/2 cup sherry
1-1/2 teaspoons garlic powder
Salt and pepper
Cooked rice

Cut steak into thin strips. In a large skillet, brown meat in olive oil. Add onions and mushrooms. Sauté until onions are tender crisp. In a bowl, blend soup, sherry, liquid from mushrooms, thyme, and garlic powder. Add salt and pepper as needed. Pour over steak. Reduce heat; cover and simmer 1 hour or until steak is tender. Serve over hot fluffy rice.

Venison Steak With Garlic-Mustard Sauce

Venison tenderloin steaks cut 1-inch thick
Salt
Coarse-ground black pepper
1 tablespoon olive oil
1 garlic clove, minced
1/3 cup onion or green onions, minced
1/2 cup brandy
1/2 cup beef broth
1/4 cup Dijon mustard

Sprinkle steaks with salt and pepper. Heat oil in a 9-inch cast iron skillet over medium-high heat. Add steaks; cook approximately 3 to 5 minutes on each side (medium-rare) or until desired-degree of doneness. Remove steaks from pan. Cover and keep warm.

Add garlic and onions to skillet; sauté for about 30 seconds. Add brandy; stir and cook for 1 minute. Add beef broth and mustard, stirring to blend in mustard. Reduce heat and cook for 2 minutes, stirring constantly. To serve, spoon 2 table-spoons sauce over each steak.

Venison Cutlets & Sour Cream Gravy

2 pounds cut venison steaks
1/3 cup all-purpose flour
1 teaspoon salt
1/4 teaspoon pepper
1 egg, beaten
2 tablespoons milk
1 cup fine dry bread crumbs
1/4 cup vegetable oil
1/2 cup sour cream
1 cup milk
2 teaspoons drained capers
Salt and pepper
1 lemon, sliced thin

With a meat mallet, pound each steak to 1/4- to 1/8-inch thick. Combine flour, salt and pepper. Coat meat with flour mixture; reserve remaining flour mixture. Combine beaten egg and milk. Dip floured cutlets in egg mixture then in bread crumbs. In a large skillet, brown the cutlet in hot oil for 2 to 3 minutes on each side or until tender and evenly browned. Remove meat to platter; keep warm. In a bowl, blend sour cream and 1 tablespoon of reserved flour mixture. Stir in the milk and capers. Pour into the skillet; cook over low heat. Stir until thickened. Season to taste with salt and pepper. Spoon some of the gravy over cutlets. Garnish with thin lemon slices. Serve remaining gravy with meat.

Venison Goulash

2 pounds venison, cut into 1-1/2-inch cubes
3 tablespoons all-purpose flour
2 tablespoons bacon drippings or vegetable oil
1 large onion, chopped fine
2 cloves garlic, minced
1 tablespoon paprika
1/2 cup red wine
4 cups boiling water
Salt and pepper to taste
1 can (6-ounce) tomato paste
1 cup sour cream

Melt bacon drippings in a Dutch oven or heavy kettle. Place flour in a small bowl or plastic zip-top bag. Coat meat in flour; shake off excess. Brown meat in bacon drippings on all sides. Add onion and garlic; cook until transparent. Add water, paprika, red wine, tomato paste, salt and pepper. Stir well to combine flavors. Cover, simmer until meat is tender, approximately 2 to 3 hours, depending on cut of meat used. Add more water or wine if necessary. Stir in sour cream, just before serving. Serve immediately with buttered noodles.

Venison Meatballs in Potato Dill Sauce

1 pound ground venison
1 egg
1 cup fresh bread crumbs
1/4 cup onion, minced
2 tablespoons dried parsley
3/4 teaspoon salt
1/4 teaspoon pepper
1/3 cup milk
2 tablespoons vegetable oil

Sauce:

1 can (10-3/4-ounce) cream of potato soup
1/2 cup milk
1/3 teaspoon dried dill weed

In medium bowl, mix first 8 ingredients. Shape mixture into 1-1/2 inch meatballs. Heat oil in a skillet over medium-high heat. Cook meatballs until well browned; drain on paper towels. Discard drippings from skillet. In same skillet over medium heat, stir in potato soup, milk and dill weed. Heat to boiling. Add meatballs, reduce heat, and cook until heated through. Serve with mashed potatoes, or atop cooked rice or buttered noodles.

Venison Meatballs with Caraway Sour Cream

Meatballs with a German flair

1 egg, slightly beaten
1/4 cup milk
1/4 cup fine dry bread crumbs
1 tablespoon fresh parsley, snipped
1/2 teaspoon salt
1/4 teaspoon poultry seasoning
Dash pepper
1 pound ground venison
1 tablespoon vegetable oil
1 can (10-1/2-ounce) beef broth
1 can (4-ounce) mushrooms, drained and chopped
1/2 cup onion, chopped
1 cup sour cream
1 tablespoon all-purpose flour
1/2 to 1 teaspoon caraway seeds

In a bowl, combine the egg, milk, bread crumbs, parsley, salt, poultry seasoning, and pepper. Add in the ground venison and mix well. Shape mixture into twenty-four 1-1/2 inch meatballs. Heat oil in skillet over medium heat; brown meatballs. Drain off any excess oil. To the skillet, add in beef broth, mushrooms, and onions. Cover, simmer for 30 minutes.

In a small bowl, combine sour cream, flour and caraway seeds; stir into meatball mixture. Cook and stir until mixture thickens. Serve meatballs and gravy over hot buttered noodles.

Venison Mincemeat I

Makes approximately 4 quarts

2 pounds ground venison
1/2 pound finely ground beef suet
4 quarts tart apples, peeled and chopped
2 pounds seedless raisins
1 pound golden raisins
1 pound currants
1 large orange, juice and grated rind
1 lemon, juice and grated rind
3-3/8 cups dark brown sugar
1-1/2 teaspoons salt
1-1/2 teaspoons ground allspice
1-1/2 teaspoons cinnamon
1-1/2 teaspoons ground cloves
1-1/2 teaspoons mace
1-1/2 teaspoons nutmeg
1 cup apple cider
1 cup brandy

In a large kettle, simmer venison and suet in 1 cup of water, covered for about 10 minutes. Add remaining ingredients, except brandy. Stir mixture to blend ingredients. Bring to a hard boil; reduce heat to low. Simmer for about 5 minutes. Stir frequently to keep from sticking to bottom of kettle. Remove kettle from stove and cool mixture. Stir in one cup of brandy. Store for use later.

For pie: Fill pastry-lined pie pan with mincemeat. Dot with 2 tablespoons butter. Adjust top crust and bake at 425 degrees for about 30 minutes.

Venison Mincemeat II

2 to 3 pounds cubed venison (amount depends on how meaty you want it)
1 pound beef suet
5 pounds apples, peeled and chopped
2 pounds raisins
2 pounds dried currants
1 quart total of red wine, apple cider, pineapple juice mixed together
    (total mixed volume in any proportion)
2-1/4 pounds brown sugar
2 tablespoons cinnamon
1 tablespoon nutmeg
1 tablespoon ground cloves
1 tablespoon ground allspice
1 tablespoon salt
1 to 1-1/2 pounds chopped walnuts
1 to 1-1/2 cups brandy
1 to 1-1/2 cups rum

In a heavy kettle, heat suet until melted. Add venison and braise until well browned. Add remaining ingredients, except brandy and rum. Simmer for 2 to 3 hours until mixture is thick. Stir frequently to keep mixture from sticking and burning. Remove from heat and cool.

When mixture has cooled sufficiently, stir in brandy and rum. Amount of brandy and rum can vary according to personal taste. Store for use later.

Venison Rollups

2-1/2 pounds cut venison steaks
6 teaspoons prepared mustard
6 bacon slices, diced
3 small dill pickles, minced
1 medium onion, minced
2 tablespoons vegetable oil
1-1/2 teaspoons salt
1/4 teaspoon pepper
1 can (8-ounce) tomato sauce
1 teaspoon sugar
1 package (8-ounce) noodles
3 tablespoons all-purpose flour
1/4 cup cold water

With a meat mallet, pound each steak 1/4 to 1/8 inch thick. Spread each piece of meat with 1 teaspoon of mustard. In a small bowl, mix bacon, pickles, and onion. Spoon this mixture along one end of each piece of meat. Roll meat up, jellyroll fashion, and tie securely with string or fasten with toothpicks.

Heat oil in a large skillet over medium heat. Brown meat rolls well on all sides. Sprinkle with salt and pepper. Add tomato sauce and sugar. Simmer, covered, 1 hour or until meat is fork tender. Turn meat rolls once during cooking time.

Cook noodles as package directs; drain and place in warm serving dish. Remove string or toothpicks from meat; place on noodles. In a bowl, blend flour and water; stir into pan juices. Cook, stirring until thickened; pour over meat and serve.

Venison Shish Kabobs

2 pounds venison, cut into 1 inch cubes
1/2 cup French dressing
2 green peppers cut into squares
1 large onion, cut into 1/2 inch pieces
1/3 pound mushroom caps

Place venison cubes in ceramic bowl and pour dressing over venison. Let marinate at least 2 hours. Remove venison, reserving marinade.

Alternate cubes, pepper squares, onion pieces and mushroom caps on skewers. Brush with marinade. Have grill at medium-high heat. Grill until done to desired-degree. Turn frequently, basting with marinade as needed.

Tip: Times are approximate – 15 minutes for rare, 20 to 25 minutes for well done.

Venison Steak & Mushroom Kabobs

Great for grilling or under the broiler

2-1/2 pounds venison cut into 2 inch pieces
2 cups (16 ounces) large fresh mushrooms, or canned mushroom caps, drained
Marinade:
1/3 cup dry red wine
1/2 cup olive oil
1 clove garlic, minced fine
1/2 teaspoon dried marjoram
1/2 teaspoon dried basil
1/2 teaspoon oregano
1 teaspoon salt
2 tablespoons ketchup
1 tablespoon cider vinegar
1 teaspoon Worcestershire sauce

In plastic zip-top bag or non-metallic bowl, combine all marinade ingredients. Add steak and mushrooms, coating with marinade. Cover bowl tightly; refrigerate for 2 hours or overnight. Drain, set meat and mushrooms aside. Put marinade in a small saucepan; heat to boiling. Reduce heat to a slow boil and cook marinade for 5 minutes. Thread meat and mushrooms alternately on skewers. Broil 3 to 4 inches from heat, or grill over hot coals. Brush marinade over kabobs. Turn kabobs occasionally until meat reaches desired-degree of doneness.

Venison Steak with Port Wine Sauce

A delicious way to prepare at home or deer camp

Venison steaks cut 1/2 to 3/4 inch thick
Salt
Coarse ground black pepper
Olive oil

Wine sauce:

2 tablespoons butter
1/8 teaspoon salt or less
4 tablespoons port wine
2 tablespoons currant jelly

Dip steaks in a shallow dish of olive oil and let excess drip off. Season steaks with salt and coarsely ground black pepper to personal taste.

One of three methods can be used to cook your steaks. The meat should be seared but slightly rare in the middle.

Method 1) Broil steaks on each side in oven using a broiler pan.

Method 2) If using a charcoal grill or wood fire, broil steaks over the hottest part of grill.

Method 3) Fry quickly in hot skillet on both sides.

In a small saucepan, combine butter, salt, port wine and currant jelly. Stir mixture over low heat until jelly melts and ingredients are blended. Pour hot sauce over venison. Serve immediately.

Substitute broth or fruit juice for wine in recipes; however, you may lose the full-bodied flavor of the dish.

Venison Stroganoff

2 pounds venison round steak cut 3/4 inch thick
2 tablespoons vegetable oil
1 large onion, peeled and chopped
1/2 teaspoon salt
1/8 teaspoon pepper
1 can (14-1/2 ounces) beef broth
1/2 pound fresh mushrooms
2 tablespoons butter
2 tablespoons quick-mixing flour
2 tablespoons tomato paste
1 cup dairy sour cream

Cut steak into strips about 1/4 inch wide and 1-1/2 inches long. Brown meat in oil in a heavy skillet. When browned, transfer meat to a 2-quart casserole dish; add onion, salt and pepper. Heat beef broth in the skillet, scraping bottom of pan to loosen particles. Pour over meat and onions. Cover, bake at 350 degrees 1-1/2 hours, stirring occasionally if meat on top becomes dry.

Toward end of cooking time, wash and slice mushrooms. Heat butter in skillet; sauté mushrooms until golden. Drain liquid from meat in casserole dish; blend in with mushrooms. Reduce heat and sprinkle in flour, stirring constantly. Cook over low heat, stirring constantly, until smooth and thickened. Add tomato paste and sour cream; blend well. Pour over meat in casserole dish. Serve over cooked noodles or cooked rice.

Venison Stuffed Cabbage Leaves

2 pounds ground venison
5 tablespoons onion, chopped
3 tablespoons butter or margarine
2 cups cooked brown rice
1 tablespoon fresh dill, chopped, or dried dill
Salt and pepper
12 large cabbage leaves
2 (8-ounce) cans tomato sauce

Melt butter in a skillet; brown venison and onion. Stir in rice, chopped dill, salt and pepper to taste. Place 12 large cabbage leaves in boiling water for 1 minute. Drain; pat dry with paper toweling. Place equal portions of meat mixture in center of each leaf. Fold leaf over and secure with toothpicks. Spray a baking dish with non-stick cooking spray; place filled leaves secured-side down in dish. Pour tomato sauce over leaves. Bake in a 325-degree oven about 45 minutes.

Venison Swiss Steak

1-1/2 pounds venison round steak cut 1-1/2 inches thick
1 cup all-purpose flour
3 to 4 tablespoons vegetable oil
3 large onions, chopped
1 rib celery, diced
Salt and pepper
1 can (14-1/2-ounce) diced tomatoes, undrained
2 tablespoons Worcestershire sauce
1 teaspoon dried basil leaves

Dredge venison steak in flour; season both sides with salt and pepper. Heat oil in a cast-iron skillet over medium-high heat. Brown steak on both sides. Add onions, celery, tomatoes, Worcestershire sauce, and basil to the pan. Cover tightly.

With an electric skillet, set temperature to simmer range. Cook about 1-1/2 hours or until meat is tender.

To cook in the oven, cover skillet with aluminum foil. Bake at 350 degrees about 1-1/2 hours or until meat is tender.

Venison Tenderloin Stuffed with Spinach and Mushrooms

A taste-tantalizing combination

4 pounds venison tenderloin
1/2 cup butter
1 pound fresh mushrooms, sliced
1 package (10-ounce) frozen spinach, thawed and squeezed dry
3/4 cup onion, diced
1/2 cup celery, diced
1 teaspoon salt
1/8 teaspoon pepper
1/2 teaspoon dried sage
1/2 teaspoon dried thyme
2 tablespoons flour
1 tablespoon olive oil
1 small garlic clove, minced
Salt and pepper to taste

Preheat oven to 325 degrees. Slit tenderloin beginning on one side and cutting toward the other, being careful not to cut through other side.

Mince spinach very fine. Melt butter in a skillet. Sauté mushrooms until lightly browned. Add 1/2 cup spinach, onion, celery, salt, pepper, sage, and thyme. Sauté until vegetables are tender. Blend in flour and cook 1 minute; cool mixture. Stuff mixture into slit. Lace string around tenderloin to close opening.

Lay tenderloin in shallow roasting pan. Rub outer surface of meat with olive oil. Sprinkle with minced garlic and any remaining spinach. Season with additional salt and pepper.

Roast 1-1/2 hours at 325 degrees, or until meat thermometer registers desired-degree of doneness. To serve, remove string, slice and place on a heated platter. Spoon any pan juices over meat.

Venison Wild Rice Casserole

2/3 cup uncooked wild rice
1 can (14-1/2-ounce) beef broth
2 tablespoons butter or margarine
1-1/2 to 2 pounds venison steak, cubed
1 large onion, chopped
1 cup celery, diced
1 can (10-1/2 ounces) cream of mushroom soup
1 can (10-1/2 ounces) cream of chicken soup
1/4 cup white wine
1/4 cup water
3 tablespoons soy sauce
Salt and pepper to taste

In a medium saucepan, add the wild rice and beef broth. Cook wild rice until grains have split slightly open. Drain off excess liquid. Fluff rice with fork.

Melt butter in skillet; brown venison cubes, onions and celery. Combine soups, wine, water, and soy sauce in a bowl. Spray a casserole dish with cooking spray. Combine wild rice, soup mixture, meat and vegetables in casserole dish. Season with salt and pepper. Cover; cook at 325 degrees for 1 to 1-1/2 hours or until meat is tender.

Weeknight Jiffy Venison

1-1/2 pounds venison steak, cut 3/4 inch thick
2 tablespoons olive oil
2 medium zucchini, cut into 1 inch chunks
1 green pepper, seeded, cut into chunks
1 large onion, cut into thick wedges
3 ribs celery, cut into 1 inch slices
3 cloves garlic, sliced
1 teaspoon dried rosemary
Salt and pepper
1/2 cup Zinfandel wine
1 can (14-1/2-ounce) Italian style diced tomatoes

In a large skillet or electric skillet, heat 1 tablespoon oil. Cook zucchini, green pepper, onion, celery, garlic, and rosemary over medium heat for 6 to 7 minutes, or until vegetables are just crisp-tender. Stir occasionally. Remove mixture from skillet to a bowl; set aside.

Add remaining oil to skillet; add venison. Season with salt and pepper. Cook over medium-high heat for 6 to 10 minutes, until desired doneness. Remove meat from skillet; cover and keep warm.

Add wine to skillet, stirring up browned bits. Add undrained tomatoes; bring to a boil. Boil gently, uncovered, for 5 minutes, or until slightly thickened. Return vegetables to skillet. Cook, stirring until heated through. Spoon vegetable sauce over meat to serve.

Zesty Venison Strips

1-1/2 to 2 pounds venison steak
2 to 3 tablespoons olive oil
3/4 cup green onion and tops, chopped
1 clove garlic, minced
1 (8-ounce) can Italian tomato sauce
1/4 cup Burgundy or other dry red wine
1 tablespoon vinegar
1 teaspoon brown sugar
1/2 teaspoon ground cinnamon
1/4 teaspoon salt
1/4 teaspoon ground cloves
1/4 teaspoon ground coriander
1/4 teaspoon crushed red pepper flakes

Slice venison steak diagonally across grain into 1/4 inch strips. Heat olive oil in a large nonstick skillet over medium-high heat until hot. Add venison strips, green onion and tops, and garlic; cook until venison strips are browned. Add remaining ingredients to skillet and bring to a boil. Cover, reduce heat, and simmer 1 hour or until meat is tender. Stir occasionally. Serve over hot cooked egg noodles.

Note: Have steak partially frozen for easier, even slicing.

UPLAND

BIRDS

Upland Bounty — Pheasant, Partridge, Quail & Turkey

Upland gamebirds, from a 6-ounce quail on up to the wily 20-pound turkey, provide the most varied and most delicious wild meat available. Quality and flavor, of course, depend on how they are handled after the hunt.

There are a few simple rules:

Draw the birds as soon after they are shot as is possible.

Allow body heat to dissipate quickly.

Keep birds cool until they are packaged or cooked.

Whether you pluck or skin your birds, wash the bird carefully inside and out in cold water. Remove any blood and thoroughly clean the body cavity. Also search for and remove any shot pellets you may find. Cut away any badly shot areas. Finally, drain the birds on layers of paper towel before packaging.

With small birds, such as quail, use a kitchen shears and slit down either the backbone or breastbone before washing. This makes cleaning the cavity easier. Package individual birds in plastic sandwich bags. Press out the air before sealing, and then wrap in freezer wrap.

With larger birds, wrap in double plastic bags. Double bagging will help prevent a sharp bone from puncturing the bag. Again, press out any air before sealing and then wrap in freezer wrap.

Before putting your birds into the freezer, label each package with the contents and date. This eliminates playing the game of "what is this?"

When it comes time to prepare that wild turkey, cook it exactly the same as the supermarket variety. Wild turkey meat has a fine or more delicate grain than domestic, and to my way of thinking, it is much tastier.

The age of the bird determines the cooking method. Young birds have lighter legs, soft breastbones, and flexible beaks. Dry cooking methods, such as frying, are appropriate for young birds. Older birds have darker, hard-skinned legs, brittle breastbones, and inflexible beaks. Moist cooking methods, such as stewing or braising, are appropriate for these older birds.

Whether your birds are simmered in a casserole or stuffed and roasted to a deep golden brown, you'll experience gourmet treats. Now let's get cooking.

Baked Pheasant Strips

4 pheasant breast halves, skinned and boned
1-1/2 cups Italian bread crumbs
3 tablespoons Parmesan cheese, grated
3/4 teaspoon garlic powder
1/2 cup vegetable oil

In a large plastic zip-top bag, combine bread crumbs, cheese, and garlic powder. Pour oil into a small bowl. Place a breast between two sheets of heavy plastic wrap. With a meat mallet, flatten breast meat to 1/4 inch thick; cut into 1 inch wide strips. Do the same to remainder of breasts. Dip strips in oil; place in bag with crumb mixture and toss to coat. Remove; place on a greased baking sheet. Bake at 350 degrees for 20 minutes or until golden brown. Serve with Honey Dipping Sauce. (See p. 248)

Baked Quail in Mushroom Sauce

6 quail, skin off
1/2 cup all-purpose flour
1/2 teaspoon seasoned salt
1/4 teaspoon pepper
3 tablespoons olive oil
1 can (10-3/4-ounce) cream of mushroom soup
1/2 soup can white wine
1 cup sour cream
1/4 teaspoon poultry seasoning
1 can (8-ounce) sliced mushrooms, drained

Rinse quail; pat dry inside and out. In a small bowl, combine flour, seasoned salt and pepper. Coat quail with flour mixture. Brown on both sides in hot oil in a skillet. Remove quail with a slotted spoon and place in a shallow baking dish. Combine soup, wine, sour cream, poultry seasoning and mushrooms in a bowl. Pour over quail. Cover and bake at 325 degrees for 1 hour or until quail is tender.

Baked Quail in White Wine

6 quail, dressed
4 to 5 tablespoons olive oil
1 large onion, minced
2 whole cloves
1 teaspoon peppercorns
2 cloves garlic, minced
1/2 bay leaf
2 cups white wine
1/2 teaspoon salt
1/4 teaspoon pepper
2 cups half-and-half

Heat oil in a skillet. Add onions, cloves, peppercorns, garlic, and bay leaf; cook for several minutes. Add quail and brown on all sides. Add in wine. Season with salt and pepper. Cover, simmer until birds are tender, about 30 minutes.

Remove quail to a serving dish. Strain cooking liquid and return to skillet. Stir in half-and-half; heat until bubbly. Remove; pour sauce over quail in dish.

Note: A Sauterne, Chardonnay, or Chablis wine can be used. Each will produce a different, subtle flavor.

Allow two quail per person, when serving as an entreé. One quail is appropriate for an appetizer serving.

Biscuit-Topped Turkey Stew

1 cup packaged biscuit mix
1/4 cup milk
1/4 cup onion, chopped
1/4 cup green pepper, chopped
1 clove garlic, minced
2 tablespoons vegetable oil
2 tablespoons all-purpose flour
1 teaspoon sugar
3/4 teaspoon salt
1/4 teaspoon dried sage
1/8 teaspoon pepper
1 can (16-ounce) tomatoes, undrained, cut up
2 cups cubed cooked turkey
2 cups frozen peas and carrots, thawed
1 teaspoon instant beef bouillon granules
1 teaspoon Worcestershire sauce

Stir together biscuit mix and milk until well blended. Roll out dough on floured surface to a 5-inch circle. Cut into 6 wedges; set aside.

In a saucepan, cook onion, green pepper, and garlic in hot oil until onion is tender. Stir in flour, sugar, salt, sage, and pepper. Blend in tomatoes, meat, vegetables, bouillon granules, and Worcestershire sauce. Cook and stir until thickened and boiling gently. Pour turkey mixture into a casserole dish. Immediately top with biscuit wedges. Bake, uncovered, at 400 degrees until biscuits are golden, 15 to 20 minutes.

Braised Quail in Rosemary Sauce

8 quail, skin off
Salt and pepper
Paprika
1 tablespoon butter
2 tablespoons oil
1/2 cup chicken broth
1/2 cup Sauterne wine
1/2 teaspoon fresh thyme, finely minced
1/2 teaspoon fresh rosemary, finely minced
1/4 teaspoon pepper
1/8 cup quick-mixing flour
1/2 cup half-and-half

Season each bird with salt, pepper and paprika. Heat butter and oil in a heavy skillet over medium heat. Brown quail on all sides. Remove and set aside. To the skillet, add chicken broth, wine, thyme and rosemary. Simmer, scrape up any particles from browning process. Return quail to skillet; cover and simmer 30 minutes or until meat is tender.

Remove quail to a heated serving dish. Cover and keep warm. Shake one-half of the quick-mixing flour into skillet juices. Stir to blend. When smooth, stir in half-and-half. Cook over high heat until mixture thickens to desired consistency. Sprinkle in more flour if necessary. Adjust seasonings. Spoon sauce over quail before serving.

Caramelized Pheasant with Sesame Craisin Sauce

6 tablespoons frozen orange juice concentrate, thawed
4 tablespoons balsamic vinegar
4 tablespoons dry sherry
2 garlic cloves, minced
4 pheasant breast halves, skin off, boned
6 tablespoons brown sugar
2 tablespoons sesame oil
1 medium onion, chopped
1/2 cup dried craisins
1 to 2 tablespoons sesame seeds, toasted
2 tablespoons green onions, minced

Combine first four ingredients in a heavy plastic zip-top bag. Flatten each pheasant breast to about 1/4 inch with flat side of a meat mallet. Put breast meat into plastic zip-top bag with the marinade. Seal and chill at least 1 hour. Remove pheasant from marinade. Save marinade.

Cook brown sugar and sesame oil in a large nonstick skillet or electric fry pan over medium-high heat (325 degrees) for several minutes; stir constantly. Add pheasant, cooking 3 to 4 minutes on each side. Add saved marinade, onion, and craisins. Cook pheasant about 10 minutes or until done. Stir and turn pheasant often.

To serve, remove pheasant and slice breast meat. Arrange slices fanned out on plate. Spoon the craisin sauce over slices. Sprinkle with sesame seeds and green onions.

*Craisins are dried cranberries.

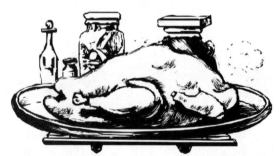

Remind family and dinner guests that they may still find pellets of shot in the meat.

Upland Birds

Charleston Quail & Creamy Grits

A taste of southern low-country cooking

8 quail, dressed, halved
1/2 cup all-purpose flour
Salt and pepper
1/8 teaspoon garlic powder
2 tablespoons butter or margarine
1 tablespoon vegetable oil
1 can (10-3/4-ounce) cream of mushroom soup, or substitute cream of celery or
    golden mushroom soup
1/4 soup can water
4 tablespoons white wine
Pinch dried rosemary

Place flour in a shallow bowl; roll quail in flour. Shake off excess. Over
medium-high heat, melt butter in skillet; add oil. Brown quail on both sides.
During browning process, season with salt, pepper, and garlic salt. Reduce heat
to simmer. Combine soup and water; pour over quail in skillet. Stir in wine.
Sprinkle rosemary over mixture. Cover; simmer for 30 minutes or until quail are
tender. Serve with prepared stone-ground grits, wild rice, or mashed potatoes.

Creamy Grits

A southern staple

2 cups water
2 cups heavy cream
1/4 pound butter
1 teaspoon salt
1/2 teaspoon white pepper
1 cup grits (not instant)

Place first 5 ingredients in a saucepan. Bring contents to a boil; add grits.
Reduce heat to simmer and simmer for 30 minutes. Stir frequently during cooking. Serve with quail over top of grits.

Crab-Stuffed Pheasant Rolls

4 pheasant breasts, skin off, boned, and halved
3 tablespoons butter or margarine
1/4 cup all-purpose flour
3/4 cup milk
3/4 cup chicken broth
1/2 cup dry white wine
1/4 cup onion, chopped
1 tablespoon butter or margarine
1 can (7-1/2-ounce) crab meat, drained and flaked
1 can (4-ounce) mushrooms, drained and chopped
1/2 cup saltine crackers, coarsely crumbled
2 tablespoons dried parsley
1/2 teaspoon salt
Dash pepper
1 cup shredded Swiss cheese
1/2 teaspoon paprika

Place pheasant breast between two pieces of wax paper. Lightly pound with flat side of meat mallet to make cutlet about 1/8 inch thick. Repeat with remaining breasts. Set aside.

In a saucepan, melt 3 tablespoons butter; blend in flour. Add milk, broth, and wine. Cook on low heat; stir until mixture thickens and bubbles. Set aside.

In a skillet, melt butter and cook onion until tender, but not brown. Stir in crab meat, mushrooms, cracker crumbs, parsley, salt and pepper, along with 2 tablespoons of the sauce.

Top each cutlet with 1/8 crab mixture. Fold sides in; roll up. Place seam side down in a 9- by 13-inch baking pan. Pour remaining sauce over all. Bake, covered, at 350 degrees for 1 hour or until tender. Uncover, sprinkle with cheese and paprika. Bake until cheese melts.

Creamy Pheasant Casserole

2 pheasants cut into pieces
1 can (10-3/4-ounce) cream of mushroom soup
1 can (10-3/4-ounce) cream of chicken soup
1 carton (8-ounce) whipping cream
1 can (4-ounce) mushrooms, drained
1 can (2.25-ounce) sliced black olives, drained
Salt and pepper to taste
1/8 teaspoon garlic salt
1/8 teaspoon paprika
Buttered bread crumbs

Parboil pheasants for about 10 minutes. Cool. Bone and cut meat into 1/2 inch cubes. Place in a greased casserole dish. Mix both soups, whipping cream, mushrooms, black olives, salt and pepper in a bowl. Pour mixture over pheasant, distributing evenly. Sprinkle the top with a little garlic salt and paprika. Sprinkle buttered bread crumbs over mixture.

Bake, uncovered, at 325 degrees for about 1-1/2 hours. Serve over rice or noodles.

Lori & Mike Writz, Rhinelander, WI

Crunchy Cheesy Turkey Bake

1 pound cooked wild turkey, cut into 1/2 inch cubes
2 cans (15 ounces each) mixed vegetables, drained
1 can (10-3/4-ounce) cream of mushroom soup
1 can (8-ounce) sliced water chestnuts, drained
1 cup shredded sharp cheddar cheese
3/4 cup mayonnaise
1 medium onion, finely chopped
3 celery ribs, finely chopped
Salt and pepper
1 cup coarsely crushed cheese-flavored crackers
1 cup canned French-fried onions

In a large bowl, combine all ingredients except cracker crumbs and French-fried onions. Mix well. Grease a 3-quart casserole dish and spoon mixture into it. Season with salt and pepper.

Cover and bake at 350 degrees for 60 minutes. Sprinkle cracker crumbs and French-fried onions over the top. Bake an additional 5 to 10 minutes, or until bubbly and heated through.

Deep Fried Marinated Wild Turkey

1 wild turkey, dressed
Salt and pepper
1-1/2 cups vegetable oil
2 cups real lemon juice
3 tablespoons Italian seasoning
1 teaspoon poultry seasoning
Peanut oil (for deep frying)

Rinse turkey with water, pat dry and place in a pan. Season bird inside and out with salt and pepper. Mix remaining ingredients together. Rub mixture over and inside the bird. Cover with plastic wrap and refrigerate overnight. Baste turkey occasionally with any of the mixture that accumulates on bottom of pan.

When ready to deep fry turkey, remove and completely drain out all marinade. Discard marinade. Let turkey come to room temperature while oil heats in the pot. Heat oil to 350 to 365 degrees. Standard cooking time for a turkey is 3 minutes per pound. When cooked, remove, slice, and enjoy!

Divine Turkey Asparagus

2 boxes (8-ounce) turkey or chicken stuffing mix
Turkey breast, skin off, boned, cut into 8 to 10 cutlets
1 pound asparagus spears cut into 1 inch pieces, or 1 package (9-ounce) frozen
    asparagus cuts, thawed
1/2 cup white wine
1 can (10-3/4-ounce) cream of asparagus soup
3 tablespoons butter or margarine, melted
2 cups shredded 6 Italian cheeses

Prepare stuffing mix according to instructions on box. Spread stuffing on bottom of a 9- by 13-inch baking pan. Lay turkey cutlets over stuffing. Arrange asparagus spears over top of cutlets. Combine wine and asparagus soup in a bowl. Pour mixture over contents in pan. Drizzle melted butter over all. Bake in a 350-degree oven for 1 hour, or until turkey is cooked and tender. Remove from oven; sprinkle cheese over top. Return to oven; bake 5 minutes longer or until cheese melts.

Golden Raisin Pheasant

1 pheasant, dressed, skin on
3 tablespoons orange juice concentrate
Salt and pepper
1/2 teaspoon poultry seasoning
1/4 teaspoon paprika
1 orange
2 cloves garlic, peeled and cut in half
2 tablespoons parsley
3 tablespoons butter or margarine, softened
3 slices bacon
1 cup dry white wine
1/2 cup golden raisins

Combine orange juice concentrate, salt and pepper, poultry seasoning, and paprika in a bowl. Rub bird inside and out with this mixture. Cut whole orange in quarters, place in cavity of bird along with garlic and parsley.

Place bird breast side up in a shallow roasting pan. Spread butter over breast. Lay bacon slices over the breast. Cover with aluminum foil; bake at 350 degrees for 45 minutes.

Heat the wine to a boil in a small saucepan. Remove pan from heat; add golden raisins. Let stand for 45 minutes. Remove foil and pour wine mixture over pheasant. Reduce heat to 325 degrees. Bake uncovered, basting periodically, for an additional 45 to 60 minutes or until pheasant is tender.

To serve, remove orange slices and garlic from cavity of bird. Place pheasant on a serving platter. Cut pheasant breast into slices; spoon raisin sauce over slices. Serve any remaining sauce in a small bowl.

Gourmet Partridge Breasts

Gourmet-style fare without the fuss

8 to 12 partridge breast halves, skin off
1 teaspoon salt (approximately)
1 teaspoon black pepper
1 teaspoon paprika
2 tablespoons butter or margarine
6 to 8 slices bacon cut up
1 large onion, coarsely chopped
1 can (10-3/4-ounce) cream of mushroom soup
1 cup sour cream
1 pound fresh mushrooms, sliced
1 cup white wine
3 tablespoons oregano
3 cloves of garlic, chopped fine
1 tablespoon dried thyme
1 tablespoon dried rosemary
1 tablespoon dried parsley
2 tablespoons sage

Mix salt, black pepper and paprika in a small bowl. Dust breast halves with this mixture. Melt 2 tablespoons butter in a skillet and brown breasts. When browned, remove and place in a single layer in a 9- by 13-inch baking dish.

Add bacon and onions to the skillet. Fry bacon until crisp and onions are clear. Add in cream of mushroom soup, sour cream, mushrooms, wine, and spices. Stir to blend ingredients. Pour mixture over partridge breasts. Bake covered in a 250 degree oven for 2 to 2-1/2 hours or until done.

Variation: Substitute 4 to 8 pheasant breasts.

Dr. Eric Swanson, Cable, WI

Hawaiian Turkey-Sausage Kabobs

1 turkey breast half, 3 to 4 pounds
1/3 cup soy sauce
1/3 cup sherry
3 tablespoons sugar
3 tablespoons vegetable oil
1 package (8-ounce) brown-and-serve sausages
1 can (8-ounce) pineapple chunks, drained
4 to 5 green onions, cut into 1-1/2-inch pieces

Cut turkey breast half into 1 inch chunks. In a bowl, mix next four ingredients. Add turkey chunks to bowl, coating with marinade. Cover and refrigerate for 30 minutes. Cut each sausage in half crosswise.

Drain turkey chunks; save marinade. Alternately thread turkey, sausages, pineapple and green onions on skewers. Broil or grill 10 to 12 minutes or until turkey is tender, turning once. Baste kabobs frequently with marinade. Serve with Tangy Slaw. (See p. 238)

Herbed Breasted Turkey Roast

Whole turkey breast, skin on, bone in
1 stick butter or margarine
1/2 cup lemon juice
1/4 cup soy sauce
1-1/2 teaspoons seasoned salt
1-1/4 teaspoons basil leaves
1 teaspoon dried oregano
1 teaspoon poultry seasoning
3 cloves garlic, minced fine
1/2 teaspoon coarse ground pepper
1/2 teaspoon paprika
1/2 cup water

Place turkey breast on a rack in a roasting pan. Melt butter in a small saucepan, over medium-low heat. Stir in ingredients lemon juice through and including pepper; cook for 5 minutes. Brush one-half of mixture over turkey breast; set remaining mixture aside for basting. Pour water in bottom of roaster. Bake, covered, at 350 degrees, for 1 hour. Uncover; baste some of remaining mixture over breast. Keep uncovered and bake 45 minutes longer, basting with remaining mixture. Bake until meat is tender and skin is browned. Make gravy from pan drippings to serve with turkey slices.

Lemon Glazed Partridge

4 partridge, cut into serving pieces
1/3 cup all-purpose flour
1 teaspoon salt
1 teaspoon paprika
3 tablespoons lemon juice
3 tablespoons olive oil
1 chicken bouillon cube
3/4 cup boiling water
1/2 cup green onions, sliced
2 tablespoons brown sugar
1-1/2 teaspoons lemon peel, grated

In a plastic zip-top bag, combine flour, salt, and paprika. Brush partridge with lemon juice. Add partridge pieces, several at a time, to bag; shake to coat. Heat oil in a large skillet or electric fry pan; brown partridge pieces on all sides. In a cup, dissolve bouillon cube in hot water; pour over partridge. Stir in onion, brown sugar, lemon peel, and any remaining lemon juice. Cover; reduce heat. Cook over low heat until partridge is tender, 45 to 60 minutes. To serve, spoon pan drippings over partridge.

Variation: Substitute 1 pheasant or 8 quail.

Moist Garlic Partridge

6 to 8 partridge breasts, skin off, boned
1/3 cup butter or margarine, melted
2 cloves garlic, minced or 1 teaspoon garlic powder
1/4 to 1/2 teaspoon salt (optional)
1/2 cup seasoned bread crumbs
1/4 teaspoon thyme
1/4 cup finely shredded cheddar cheese
2 tablespoons grated Parmesan cheese
Dash pepper

In a shallow bowl, combine butter and garlic. In another bowl, combine bread crumbs, thyme, cheeses and pepper. Dip each breast in butter mixture, roll in bread mixture. Press mixture on the breast.

Coat a 9- by 13-inch pan with cooking spray. Arrange breasts in pan. Cover and bake at 350 degrees for 15 minutes. Uncover, continue to bake for an additional 30 to 35 minutes or until tender.

Partridge Almondine

Mouth-watering aromas will be the only dinner call needed

3 cups cooked partridge, cubed
1 can (10-3/4-ounce) cream of chicken or mushroom soup
1 can (8-ounce) water chestnuts, drained and sliced (optional)
1 can (4-ounce) mushroom stems and pieces, drained
2/3 cup mayonnaise or salad dressing
1/2 cup celery, chopped
1/2 cup onion, chopped
1/2 cup dairy sour cream
1 can (8-ounce) refrigerated quick crescent dinner rolls
2/3 cup shredded natural Swiss or American pasteurized processed cheese
1/2 cup slivered or sliced almonds
2 to 4 tablespoons butter or margarine, melted

Combine first eight ingredients in a large saucepan. Cook over medium heat until mixture is hot and bubbly; pour into an ungreased 9- by 13-inch baking dish.

Separate crescent dough into two rectangles. Place rectangles over hot partridge mixture. Combine cheese, almonds, and butter; spread over dough. Bake at 375 degrees for 20 to 25 minutes until crust is deep golden brown. Serve immediately. Serves 4 to 6.

Note: Because mayonnaise is used, be sure to refrigerate any leftovers.

Variation: Follow recipe above, substituting cooked pheasant breasts or rabbit.

Partridge Breasts in Madeira Sauce

3 partridge breasts, halved and boned
1/3 cup all-purpose flour
1 teaspoon salt
1/2 teaspoon pepper
1/4 cup butter
1/4 cup oil
1 cup cooked wild rice
2 tablespoons green onions, finely chopped
2 cans (8-ounce) sliced mushrooms, drained
1/2 cup Madeira wine
1 cup heavy cream, scalded

Cut breasts lengthwise into 1/2 inch thick slices. Combine flour, salt and pepper in a bowl. Dredge breast slices in flour. Heat butter and oil in heavy skillet, brown breast pieces on both sides.

Butter a shallow baking dish. Place wild rice on bottom of dish. Arrange browned breast pieces on top of rice. Add onions to skillet drippings, cook until tender. Add mushrooms and cook five minutes longer. Stir in the Madeira. Add scalded cream; bring mixture to a boil. Remove immediately; season with salt and pepper. Pour over breast slices and bake at 350 degrees 15 to 20 minutes or until heated thoroughly.

Partridge Deluxe

A family favorite for many years.

3 partridge, skin off, cut into serving pieces
1 egg, slightly beaten
1/2 cup milk
Salt and pepper
Dash of garlic salt
1/4 cup butter
1/2 cup vegetable oil
1 cup all-purpose flour
1/3 cup dried parsley flakes
1 can (10-3/4-ounce) golden mushroom soup
1 cup water

Beat egg in a bowl. Add milk, salt, pepper, and garlic salt, blending all ingredients. Place butter and oil in a skillet and heat. Dip partridge in egg mixture, and roll in flour. Shake off any excess flour. Place partridge in skillet, brown on all sides. Remove partridge when browned, place in a single layer in a 9- by 13-inch pan. Stir soup and water into pan drippings. Spoon mixture over partridge. Cover, bake for one hour at 350 degrees or until tender.

Variation: Substitute pheasant.

Partridge Stroganoff

Not your typical stroganoff taste.

2 partridge, skin off, cut into serving pieces
6 bacon slices
1 can (10-3/4-ounce) cream of chicken soup
1/2 soup can water
1 can (8-ounce) sliced mushrooms, drained
1 medium onion, chopped
1/2 teaspoon dried thyme
2 tablespoons white wine
1/8 to 1/4 teaspoon garlic powder
Salt and pepper to taste
1/2 carton sour half-and-half
Crumbled bacon pieces

In a large skillet, fry bacon until crisp. Remove to a bowl. Brown partridge pieces in pan drippings. Blend water and soup in a small bowl. Pour over partridge in frying pan. Add mushrooms, onion, white wine and seasonings.

Cover pan, reduce heat and simmer for 1 to 1-1/2 hours until meat is tender. Turn pieces over and stir occasionally. Before serving, remove meat to serving dish. Add sour half-and-half into pan juices, stirring to blend. Heat until hot, but do not have mixture come to boiling point. Pour gravy over meat. Serve over egg noodles or rice. Sprinkle crumbled bacon pieces on top as garnish.

Partridge with Vegetables and Alfredo Sauce

2 to 3 partridge, skin off, breasted and halved
2 tablespoons olive oil
1 jar (1 pound 10-ounce) Alfredo Pasta Sauce
1 cup broccoli, bite size pieces
1 cup cauliflower, bite size pieces
1/4 teaspoon chicken bouillon granules
Salt and pepper
Parmesan cheese
Angel Hair pasta

Cut breasts into cubes. Heat olive oil in a skillet; brown cubed meat until tender.

Empty Alfredo pasta sauce into a large saucepan. Add in browned partridge, broccoli, cauliflower, and chicken granules. Salt and pepper to taste. Simmer mixture until broccoli and cauliflower are tender.

Prepare angel hair pasta according to package instructions. Drain and rinse. Serve partridge Alfredo sauce over pasta. Sprinkle with Parmesan cheese.

Variation: Substitute pheasant.

Partridge with Poppy Seed Noodles

3 partridge, breasted, halved, boned
2 tablespoons butter or margarine
1 medium onion, chopped
1/2 green pepper, minced
1 can (8-ounce) sliced mushrooms, drained
1 package broad size noodles
3 to 4 tablespoons butter or margarine
1 tablespoon poppy seeds
1/4 teaspoon chicken bouillon granules
Salt and pepper
Garlic salt

Cut partridge breasts into small cubes. Melt butter in a skillet. Add cubed meat; fry until tender. Add more butter to skillet if needed; sauté onions and pepper until tender. Add mushrooms to skillet and heat.

Prepare noodles in a saucepan, according to instructions on the package. Drain and rinse. Melt 3 to 4 tablespoons butter in the saucepan. Return noodles to saucepan, sprinkle with poppy seeds; add in meat, vegetables, and bouillon. Stir all ingredients to blend flavors. Season with salt, pepper, and garlic salt to taste. Serve.

Variation: Substitute pheasant.

Partridge with Fresh Thyme Sauce

It's thyme to dress up partridge

2 to 3 partridge, breasted and halved
Flour, quick-mixing
1/4 cup butter or margarine
2 garlic cloves, minced
3 tablespoons dry sherry
3/4 cup chicken broth
1/2 cup milk
1/4 cup half-and-half
2 tablespoons fresh thyme
Salt and pepper to taste

Place each breast inside plastic baggie. Use flat side of meat mallet or edge of a saucer to gently pound meat to a 1/4 inch thickness. Coat partridge breasts with flour.

Melt butter in a large skillet. Sauté breasts with garlic over low to medium heat, until golden brown and cooked through. Remove breasts, set aside in a covered dish to keep warm. Add sherry and chicken broth to the skillet. Cook and stir until about half of the liquid has evaporated. Over very low heat, add in milk, cream, thyme, salt and pepper; stirring to mix. Lightly shake in quick-mixing flour; enough to just thicken. Stir mixture. Sauce should not be thick. To serve, place breasts on individual plates and spoon sauce over each breast.

Variation: Substitute pheasant breasts.

Partridge with Velvety Dijon Mustard Sauce

4 partridge breast halves, boned
1 tablespoon cooking oil
2 cups fresh mushrooms, sliced
1/2 cup onion, chopped
1/2 cup chicken broth
1/4 cup evaporated milk
1-1/2 teaspoons all-purpose flour
1 tablespoon dry sherry
1-1/2 teaspoons Dijon-style mustard
Hot cooked pasta

Flatten breast halves with flat side of a meat mallet to about 1/4 inch thick. Heat oil in skillet over medium heat. Cook breasts in hot skillet about 5 minutes on each side to brown evenly. Remove from skillet. Add mushrooms and onion. Cook until vegetables are tender. Stir in broth; return partridge to skillet and bring to a boil. Reduce heat, cover and simmer for about 15 to 20 minutes or until partridge is tender. Remove partridge to a covered dish.

Stir together evaporated milk and flour. Add to liquid in skillet; stir until mixture comes to a rolling boil. Continue to cook and stir one minute more. Stir in sherry and mustard. Return partridge breasts to skillet to reheat. Serve breasts on a bed of pasta with sauce spooned over all.

Variation: Substitute pheasant or quail.

*Pressure cook turkey thighs and legs
for tender meat.*

Partridge Wontons

An out-of–the-ordinary appetizer

2 to 3 partridge, dressed (enough to make 1 cup diced, cooked meat)
4 green onions, diced
1 cup cabbage, finely shredded
2 tablespoons fresh parsley, diced
2 teaspoons brown sugar
1 tablespoon Hoisin sauce
1 teaspoon sesame oil
36 wonton wrappers
Peanut oil

Parboil 2 to 3 dressed partridge until meat is tender. Remove; cool meat until you can handle it. Remove meat from bones and dice into small pieces.

Stir together first 7 ingredients. Spoon 1 teaspoon of this mixture into center of each wonton wrapper. Moisten wonton edges with water. Bring corners together, pressing to seal.

Heat peanut oil in a Dutch oven, small deep fryer, or electric skillet to 375 degrees. Fry wontons in batches until golden on all sides. Remove and drain on wire racks over paper towels. Serve immediately with Hoisin Peanut Dipping Sauce (see p. 247) or Sweet Tangy Mustard Sauce (see p. 252).

Pecan Pheasant Breasts

4 pheasant breast halves, skin off, boned
3 tablespoons honey
2 tablespoons Dijon mustard
3 tablespoons finely chopped pecans

Place pheasant breasts between 2 pieces of heavy-duty plastic wrap. Flatten to 1/4-inch thickness using a meat mallet or side of a saucer. Combine honey and mustard in small bowl. Spread on both sides of pheasant, and dredge in pecans. Arrange in a lightly greased 8-inch square baking dish. Bake, uncovered, at 325 degrees for 30 to 45 minutes, or until pheasant breasts are tender. Serve with Cranberry Ketchup (see p. 242) or Red Raisin Sauce (see p. 251).

Penne Pheasant in Tomato Sauce

An elegant entrée

1 pheasant, dressed, skin off
2 tablespoons butter or margarine
1 can (28-ounce) diced Italian tomatoes, undrained
1/4 cup fresh basil, chopped
Salt and pepper to taste
1/2 cup vodka
6 tablespoons whipping cream
1 pound penne pasta

Parboil or pressure cook pheasant until tender. When meat has cooled, remove meat from bones and cube. Should have 3 cups cooked pheasant.

Melt butter in large heavy skillet over medium heat. Add tomatoes and bring to a boil. Reduce heat, add chopped basil and simmer 10 minutes. Season with salt and pepper. Add vodka and cream. Bring to a boil; boil mixture 3 minutes. Add cubed pheasant and simmer 5 minutes, stirring occasionally, until heated through.

Cook pasta according to directions on package. Remove when pasta is tender but firm to the bite. Drain well. Add pasta to sauce in skillet. Stir to combine and heat.

Variation: Substitute partridge or rabbit.

Pheasant Alexandra

A delicious entrée to serve family and friends

2 pheasants, skin off, dressed and halved lengthwise
Salt and pepper
4 tablespoons butter or margarine
3/4 cup tomatoes, peeled and chopped
1/2 cup dry white wine
1/4 cup green onion, sliced
2 tablespoons fresh parsley, snipped
1/4 teaspoon dried thyme
1 tablespoon all-purpose flour
1/2 cup light cream
Hot cooked rice

Season pheasant halves with salt and pepper. In skillet, brown pheasant in butter on both sides. In a bowl, combine tomato, wine, onion, parsley, and thyme; pour over pheasant in skillet. Cover and simmer for one hour or until tender.

Remove pheasant to warm serving dish. Measure liquid from skillet into a 1 cup measure. If necessary, add water to make 3/4 cup liquid; return to skillet. Blend flour and cream together. Pour cream mixture into skillet. Cook, stirring constantly until thickened and bubbly. Serve one-half pheasant per person. Lay pheasant on a bed of hot rice. Spoon sauce over pheasant and rice.

Variation: Substitute 4 partridge for pheasant. Proceed with recipe same as above.

Pheasant Cacciatore

1 pheasant, dressed, skin off, cut into serving pieces
2 teaspoons olive oil
1 medium onion, chopped
3 garlic cloves, minced
2 cans (8-ounce) sliced mushrooms, drained
1 can (14-1/2-ounce) diced tomatoes, undrained
1 green bell pepper, seeded and diced
3/4 cup diced celery
1/2 cup Italian tomato paste
1 teaspoon dried oregano
1/4 teaspoon black pepper
Hot cooked spaghetti

Heat oil in a large nonstick skillet. Add pheasant pieces and brown thoroughly on all sides. Remove from skillet to a plate. Sauté onion and garlic, until onion is softened, approximately 5 minutes. Add tomatoes, mushrooms, bell pepper, celery, tomato paste, oregano and black pepper. Bring to a slow boil, stirring as necessary. Reduce heat to simmer; return pheasant to skillet. Cover, continue simmering mixture until pheasant is tender. Stir mixture occasionally. To serve, place pheasant on a bed of spaghetti with sauce.

Pheasant Kiev

6 pheasant breast halves, skin off, boned
3/4 cup butter or margarine, softened
1 tablespoon parsley, chopped
1 tablespoon green onions, minced fine
1/8 teaspoon pepper
1/2 teaspoon salt
1/2 cup Prosciutto ham, chopped
1/4 cup all-purpose flour
1 teaspoon salt
1 egg
1 tablespoon water
3/4 cup dried bread crumbs
Salad oil

In small bowl, combine butter, parsley, onions, pepper, and 1/2 teaspoon salt. Form into a patty 4-1/2 inches by 3 inches; freeze.

With flat side of meat mallet or round edge of saucer, pound each breast until 1/4-inch thick. Divide Prosciutto into six equal portions; place on each breast. Cut firm butter patty into six 3/4-inch by 3-inch strips. Place one strip in center of each breast. Roll up, bringing wider edge of breast over mixture to enclose. Secure with toothpicks.

Mix flour and 1 teaspoon salt; set aside. In a bowl, beat egg and water. Place crumbs in another bowl. Coat each pheasant roll with flour; dip into egg, then cover with bread crumbs. Lay pheasant rolls in a single layer on a cookie sheet. Cover with wax paper; refrigerate 1 to 2 hours to allow bread crumbs to dry out.

In a large saucepan or deep fryer, heat 3 inches oil to 300 degrees on deep fat thermometer. Lower in 2 to 3 breasts. Fry 15 minutes or until browned and firm. Do not pierce. Drain; remove toothpicks. Place in a shallow baking pan and keep rolls warm in a 200-degree oven. Fry remainder of rolls. Serve.

Variation: Substitute partridge breasts allowing 1 to 2 per person, depending on size.

Pheasant Loaf

4 cups ground cooked pheasant
1 cup milk
1 cup chicken broth
1 teaspoon salt
1/2 teaspoon pepper
2 tablespoons minced onion
2 eggs, lightly beaten
2 cups fresh bread crumbs
1/4 teaspoon dried marjoram
1 jar prepared chicken gravy

Mix all ingredients together in a bowl. Spray a loaf pan with cooking spray. Pour pheasant mixture into pan and spread evenly. Bake at 375 degrees for 1 hour.

Heat chicken gravy and serve over pheasant loaf slices.

Variation: Substitute cooked wild turkey, rabbit.

Pheasant-Rice Bake

1 pheasant, breasted, skin off
2 tablespoons butter or margarine
1 can (10-3/4-ounce) cream of chicken soup
1 cup milk
1 envelope dry onion soup mix
1 can (4-ounce) chopped mushrooms
1 cup regular rice, uncooked
1 package (10-ounce) frozen peas and carrots, thawed

Parboil pheasant for about 10 minutes. Cool. Bone and cut meat into 1/2 inch cubes. Quickly brown pheasant cubes in a skillet with butter. In bowl, stir together mushroom soup, milk, soup mix, and undrained mushrooms. Stir pheasant cubes, uncooked rice, and thawed vegetables into remaining soup mixture. Turn rice mixture into a greased casserole dish. Cover tightly with foil. Bake at 375 degrees until rice is tender, about 1-1/2 hours.

Variation: Substitute 2 to 3 partridge.

Pheasant with Sauerkraut

1 pheasant dressed, cut into serving pieces

Marinade:

1 cup white wine
2 cups hot water
1 medium onion, chopped
1/4 teaspoon ground cloves
2 cardamon seeds, crushed

Combine all marinade ingredients in a bowl. Place pheasant in a large plastic zip-top bag and pour in marinade. Seal tightly. Refrigerate and marinate overnight.

3 to 4 tablespoons vegetable oil
Salt and pepper
Sauerkraut, about 3-1/3 cups
2 cups beef broth
1/2 teaspoon caraway seeds
1 cup dry white wine
3 tablespoons gin
Sausage links

Remove pheasant pieces from marinade. Discard marinade. In a skillet, brown pheasant in vegetable oil. Season with salt and pepper. When pieces are well browned, remove and set aside.

Drain sauerkraut and place in a saucepan. Add beef broth, caraway seeds, white wine, and gin. Simmer for 1 hour. Meanwhile, brown sausage links in skillet; drain off any accumulated grease. Cut links into bite-size pieces; add to sauerkraut mixture.

Spray a casserole dish with nonstick cooking spray. Place pheasant pieces on bottom, top with prepared sauerkraut mixture. Cover. Bake at 350 degrees until meat is tender, about 30 minutes to one hour.

Pheasant-Ham Rolls with Sauce

An easy dish to use up leftover pheasant

1 cup cooked pheasant, chopped
1 cup cooked wild rice
4 tablespoons butter or margarine, melted
12 thick slices ham
1 can (4-ounce) mushrooms, chopped
4 tablespoons butter or margarine
4 tablespoons quick-mixing flour
2 cups chicken broth
Salt and pepper

In a bowl, combine pheasant, wild rice, and butter. Lay ham slices flat. Spoon mixture onto individual ham slices in equal portions. Roll up ham. Tie with string or fasten with skewers or toothpicks to hold the roll. Spray a baking dish with vegetable spray; arrange rolls in a single layer.

In a skillet, sauté mushrooms in butter. Stir in flour; add chicken broth. Blend until smooth. Stir mixture until thick and hot. Add salt and pepper, if needed. Pour sauce over rolls. Bake in a 325-degree oven for 25 minutes.

Quail Cabbage Rolls

4 quail, dressed
Salt and pepper
4 cups cabbage, finely shredded
4 slices bacon, cooked crisp and crumbled
8 large cabbage leaves
2 tablespoons butter or margarine
1 cup chicken broth
2 large Granny Smith apples, cored and diced
1/4 teaspoon dried thyme
1/4 teaspoon dried tarragon
1/4 teaspoon caraway seeds

Lightly salt and pepper quail. Combine shredded cabbage and bacon; stuff 1/4 of the mixture in cavity of each bird. Wrap each quail in cabbage leaves using as many as needed per bird. Tie with string. Lay bird rolls in a large skillet on top of stove.

In a saucepan, combine remaining ingredients and simmer for 5 minutes. Pour over bird rolls; bring contents to a boil. Reduce heat, cover and simmer 25 to 30 minutes until tender. Remove string and cabbage leaves. Serve with juices from skillet.

Note: Prepare two quail per person.

Quick Stuffed Partridge or Pheasant Breasts

Dinner in the fast lane

8 boneless partridge breast halves
1 package (6-ounce) bread stuffing or cornmeal stuffing mix
1-2/3 cups canned chicken broth
8 slices bacon

Prepare stuffing mix as directed on package, except substitute chicken broth in place of water.

Lay four breasts on bottom of a baking pan. Spoon equal amounts of stuffing on top breasts. Top with the remaining four breasts. Wrap each breast packet with 2 slices of bacon; secure with toothpicks. Cover with aluminum foil. Bake at 325 degrees for 40 to 50 minutes. Remove foil and continue to bake until meat is tender. If breast meat begins to brown too much, recover with foil. Serve with Onion Velvet sauce (see p. 249).

Roast Pheasant and Pork Dressing

2 pheasants, dressed
1/2 pound ground lean pork
2 cups bread crumbs
1/4 cup canned beef gravy or brown sauce
1/2 teaspoon sage
6 slices bacon
1/8 cup water
2 cups chicken broth
1/2 cup celery, chopped
1 medium onion, sliced
1 large carrot, diced
1/4 teaspoon ground allspice

Sprinkle pheasant cavity and outside with salt and pepper. Brown pork in a skillet. Drain off any grease and discard. Mix pork with bread crumbs, beef gravy or brown sauce, and sage. Stuff birds with mixture. Truss the birds. Lay slices of bacon over breasts; tying in place if needed.

Place birds on a rack in a shallow roasting pan. Add 1/8 cup water. Cover; roast 30 minutes at 350 degrees. Remove cover. Add chicken broth, celery, onion, carrot, and allspice. Bake, uncovered, about 1 hour longer, or until tender. Baste frequently with liquid in pan. To brown birds, remove bacon 10 minutes before end of roasting time.

Transfer birds to a warm platter and keep warm. Strain juices from roaster into a saucepan. Remove as much surface fat as possible; discard. Measure amount of liquid left. For each cup liquid, combine 1 tablespoon all-purpose flour and 2 tablespoons water. Bring liquid to a boil; stir in flour mixture. Continue stirring until thickened. Serve gravy with pheasants.

Sautéed Breasts of Partridge

8 partridge breast halves, skin off
1 lemon cut in half, juiced
Salt and pepper
3/4 cup all-purpose flour
1/4 teaspoon dried parsley flakes
1 tablespoon olive oil
1 tablespoon butter

Between two sheets of wax paper, flatten partridge breasts with flat side of meat mallet to 1/4-inch thick. Rub each side with lemon juice; sprinkle with salt and pepper. Mix flour and parsley in a small bowl. Coat each breast in flour, shaking off excess. Set aside until flour no longer appears white on the breasts, about 10 minutes.

Heat olive oil and butter in a skillet over medium heat. Sauté partridge breasts about 4 minutes on each side or until golden brown. Remove to heated serving platter. Spoon heated Mustard Fruits (see p. 248) over breasts prior to serving.

Sauterne Partridge

2 to 3 partridge cut into serving pieces
2 tablespoons olive oil
1/4 cup all-purpose flour
Salt and pepper
1 can (10-3/4-ounce) cream of mushroom soup
1/4 cup water
1 can (8-ounce) sliced mushrooms, drained
1 medium onion, chopped
3 to 4 tablespoons Sauterne wine
1/8 teaspoon dried rosemary
Dash poultry seasoning
Salt and pepper to taste

Heat olive oil in a skillet. Mix flour, salt and pepper in a bowl. Dust partridge pieces with flour mixture; brown in skillet. Combine water and soup in a small bowl and pour over partridge in skillet. Add mushrooms, onion, wine and seasonings.

Cover pan, reduce heat and simmer for 1 hour or until meat is tender. Turn pieces over occasionally; stir mixture. Serve over egg noodles or wild or white rice.

Sesame Pheasant Strips

A great make-ahead appetizer

1 cup sour cream
2 tablespoons lemon juice
2 teaspoons celery salt
2 teaspoons Worcestershire sauce
1/4 teaspoon salt
1/4 teaspoon pepper
2 garlic cloves, minced fine
3 whole pheasant breasts, skinned, halved, boned
1 cup dry bread crumbs
1/4 teaspoon dried Italian seasoning
1/3 cup sesame seeds
1/4 cup butter or margarine, melted

Cut pheasant breasts crosswise into 1/2-inch pieces. In a large bowl, combine sour cream, lemon juice, celery salt, Worcestershire sauce, salt, pepper, and garlic; mix well. Add pheasant to mixture; coat pheasant well. Cover; refrigerate at least 8 hours or overnight.

Lightly spray a 15- by 10-inch jelly roll pan with cooking spray. In a bowl, combine bread crumbs, Italian seasoning, and sesame seeds. Remove pheasant strips from sour cream mixture; roll in crumb mixture, coating evenly. Arrange in a single layer in pan. Spoon margarine evenly over pheasant. Bake at 350 degrees for 40 to 45 minutes, or until pheasant is tender and golden brown. Serve with Sweet Tangy Mustard Sauce (see p. 252).

Skillet Partridge & Brown Rice

4 partridge breasts, skin off, halved
1 tablespoon olive oil
1 can (10-3/4-ounce) cream of chicken soup
1-1/2 cups water
1/4 teaspoon poultry seasoning
1/8 teaspoon garlic powder
1/8 teaspoon paprika
1/4 teaspoon pepper
1-1/2 cups uncooked instant brown rice
1 cup frozen peas

Place breasts between two pieces of wax paper. Pound each breast with the flat side of a meat mallet to 1/4-inch thick. In a large skillet, heat oil on medium heat. Brown breasts on both sides for 7 to 9 minutes. Remove with a slotted spoon; set aside.

In a bowl, combine soup, water, poultry seasoning, garlic powder, paprika, and pepper. Pour mixture into skillet; bring to a gentle boil. Stir in rice and peas. Lay breasts on top of rice. Reduce heat to a simmer. Cover, cook for 20 to 30 minutes, until both meat and rice are tender. Stir occasionally during cooking.

Skillet Pheasant with Mushrooms

2 pheasants, skin off, cut into serving pieces
1/2 cup all-purpose flour
Salt and pepper
2 tablespoons butter or margarine
2 cups fresh mushrooms, sliced
1/4 cup butter
1 cup white wine
3/4 cup green onions, chopped
3 tablespoons lemon juice
1/2 cup chicken broth

Combine flour, salt, and pepper in a medium-sized bowl. Lightly dust pheasant pieces in flour mixture. Melt butter in an electric skillet. Brown pheasant on all sides. Remove and set aside. Sauté mushrooms in pan drippings. Return pheasant back to skillet.

Melt 1/4 cup butter in a small saucepan. Combine wine, onion, lemon juice, and broth in with the butter. Pour this mixture over pheasants. Cover skillet. Set heat gauge to simmer. Cook for one hour or until meat is tender.

Variation: Substitute partridge.

Smothered Golden Quail

8 quail, dressed
3 tablespoons olive oil
2 tablespoons butter or margarine
1 cup green onions, chopped
1 pound fresh mushrooms, sliced
1/4 teaspoon garlic powder
1 can (10-3/4-ounce) golden mushroom soup
1/4 cup water
4 to 6 tablespoons dry sherry

In a skillet, sauté quail in olive oil until browned on both sides. Add butter, onions, mushrooms, and sauté until just tender. Mix the can of golden mushroom soup with 1/4 cup water and stir into skillet. Add sherry, the amount depending on taste. Cover and simmer for 20 to 30 minutes until quail is tender. Serve over rice or noodles.

Stuffed Burgundy Wild Turkey

1 (10-pound) wild turkey
6 to 8 slices bacon
1 cup onion, chopped
1/2 cup celery, chopped
1/2 cup water
1 package herb-seasoned cornbread stuffing mix
3/4 to 1 cup chicken broth
1 cup burgundy wine (use 1/2-cup increments)
Melted butter
Additional bacon slices (optional)

Brown 6 to 8 slices bacon in a skillet until crisp. Remove and set aside. Sauté onion and celery in bacon drippings until brown. Add 1/2 cup chicken broth to skillet; simmer for 5 minutes.

In a mixing bowl, combine stuffing mix, 1/4 cup chicken broth, 1/2 cup burgundy wine, onion mixture and crumbled bacon. Mix well. Add more chicken broth if mixture is too dry. Stuff turkey. Place turkey on a rack in roasting pan. Brush whole bird, including drumsticks, with melted butter. Place several slices of bacon across the breast. Pour a little of the chicken broth from the skillet in bottom of roaster. Cover and bake at 300 degrees for about 4-1/2 hours. Baste turkey often with melted butter and chicken broth from skillet. Insert meat thermometer in breast meat and check for doneness.

After 4-1/2 hours, pour remaining 1/2 cup wine over turkey. Bake uncovered for an additional 40 minutes basting every 10 minutes. Let stand for 10 minutes before slicing.

Stuffed Roast Pheasant

1 pheasant, dressed
1/2 pound bulk sausage meat
1 tart green apple, peeled, cored, and chopped
1/4 cup fresh parsley, chopped
1 egg, well beaten
Salt and pepper
3 slices of bacon
1/2 cup sherry
1 tablespoon red currant jelly
1-1/2 tablespoons fresh lemon juice

Wash pheasant and pat dry. Mix sausage meat with apple, parsley, and egg. Season with salt and pepper. Stuff bird with this mixture. Put bird on a rack, breast side up, in a shallow roasting pan. Cover breast of bird with bacon. Roast at 350 degrees for 1 hour, or until bird is almost tender. Pour off excess fat.

Combine sherry, currant jelly, and lemon juice; pour over bird. Baste with pan juices several times and continue roasting for 15 to 30 minutes, or until bird is tender.

Succulent Grilled Turkey Breast

Whole turkey breast, skin on, bone in
Poultry Dry Rub (see p. 250)
1/2 cup safflower oil
1 tablespoon soy sauce
1 teaspoon seasoned salt

Preheat grill to medium heat.

Wash breast and pat dry. Slide your hand between the skin and breast meat to create an opening or pocket. Make the Poultry Dry Rub recipe; rub this mixture over breast meat. Be careful not to detach all the skin from breast meat along the sides. Place turkey in an aluminum foil pan, place on grill rack. Cover and grill turkey.

Combine oil, soy sauce and seasoned salt. Use this mixture as a basting agent during grilling, basting turkey occasionally. Also baste with any pan juices.

Insert meat thermometer in breast meat and check for doneness. Do not overcook or meat will become dry. When done, remove, slice, serve, and enjoy.

Note: Save turkey legs to use in a casserole recipe.

Sunday Pheasant Casserole

1 or 2 pheasants, cut into serving pieces
1/2 cup all-purpose flour
3 tablespoons olive oil
6 cups packaged seasoned bread cubes
1 onion, chopped
3 ribs celery, diced
1/2 cup melted butter or margarine
1 can (10-3/4-ounce) cream of chicken soup, divided
1 can (2.25-ounce) sliced black olives, drained
Salt and pepper

Dredge pheasant in flour seasoned with salt and pepper. Heat olive oil in a skillet; brown pieces on each side. In a bowl, combine bread cubes, onion, celery, butter, 1/2 cup undiluted soup, and black olives. Salt and pepper as needed. Arrange pheasant in a large pan or Dutch oven; spoon dressing over pheasant.

Make gravy from pan drippings with 2 tablespoons all-purpose flour, and enough water with the remaining 1/2 can soup to make 2 cups. Stir to mix. Pour gravy mixture over pheasant. Cover tightly. Bake in a 350 degree oven until tender, about 1-1/2 hours.

Variation: Partridge or wild turkey.

Tender Turkey Thighs & Legs

Pressure cooking does the trick for tender meat

2 each turkey thighs and legs
1-1/2 cups water
1 chicken bouillon cube
Seasoned salt
Pepper

Place turkey thighs and legs in a 4-quart pressure cooker. Add water, bouillon cube, and seasoned salt and pepper to taste. Put on lid, seal, and set control at 10 pounds of pressure. For a young turkey, cook 20 minutes after control begins to jiggle. An older turkey may require up to 30 minutes cooking time. Remove from heat; cool down cooker. Place turkey on a dish; remove all bones. Cut into serving-size pieces. Prepare gravy from liquid remaining in cooker or use a packaged turkey gravy mix. Add turkey to gravy. Serve over mashed potatoes, biscuits, or dumplings.

Turkey Breast & Vegetable Barbecue

1 turkey breast, skin on
5 carrots, peeled and sliced
5 medium potatoes, peeled and quartered

Barbecue Sauce:

3 tablespoons dark brown sugar
1 cup tomato ketchup
2 tablespoons vinegar
2 teaspoons Worcestershire sauce
1/3 cup water
2 teaspoons prepared mustard
1 medium onion, minced
1/3 cup celery, chopped fine
1 teaspoon salt
1/4 teaspoon pepper

Combine all barbecue sauce ingredients in a medium saucepan. Simmer for 15 minutes, stirring occasionally.

Rinse turkey breast; pat dry. Place in roaster, breast side up. Cover and bake in a 350 degree oven for 30 minutes. Arrange carrots and potatoes around turkey. Pour barbecue sauce over vegetables and turkey. Cover and return to oven. Bake 1-1/2 hours longer or until turkey is tender. Baste occasionally. Remove cover during the last 15 minutes of baking to thicken sauce.

Turkey Breast with Spinach-Rice Stuffing

1 whole turkey breast, boned, skin on
1 tablespoon butter or margarine
1 cup onion, minced
1-1/2 cups fresh mushrooms, sliced
3 cups cooked brown rice
2 tablespoons, fine, dry bread crumbs
2 cloves garlic, minced
1 teaspoon dried basil
1/4 teaspoon dried summer savory
1/4 teaspoon dried parsley
1/4 teaspoon paprika
1/4 teaspoon ground nutmeg
1/8 teaspoon salt
1/8 teaspoon pepper
2 egg whites, slightly beaten
1 package (10-ounce) frozen spinach, thawed, drained and chopped
3 tablespoons butter
1/2 teaspoon parsley

Lay breast skin-side down on a sheet of heavy-duty plastic wrap. Starting from center of breast, slice horizontally through thickest part of each side of breast, almost to, but not through, outer edge. Flip cut pieces over to enlarge breast. Lay another sheet of plastic wrap over breast. Flatten with a meat mallet to an even thickness.

In a large skillet, melt 1 tablespoon butter. Sauté onion and mushrooms until tender. Remove skillet from heat. Add rice, all seasonings, and spinach; mix well. Spread mixture on breast to within 2 inches of sides. Roll up jellyroll fashion, starting with short end. Secure with heavy string at evenly spaced intervals. Place, seam side down in a shallow roasting pan.

Melt 3 tablespoons butter; add parsley. Brush breast with some of the melted butter. Cover; bake at 325 degrees for 30 minutes. Remove cover; continue baking at 325 degrees for about 1-1/2 to 2 hours, or until tender. Baste frequently with remaining melted butter.

To serve, place turkey breast on serving platter. Let stand for 10 minutes before slicing. Remove string; cut into slices.

Turkey, Ham & Wild Rice Casserole

4 tablespoon butter
1/4 cup onions, chopped
1/2 cup green pepper, chopped
1/2 cup celery, chopped
1/2 pound fresh mushrooms, sliced
1 pound cooked turkey, cubed
2 to 3 cups cooked ham, cubed
1-1/2 cups cooked wild rice
1 can (10-3/4-ounce) cream of mushroom soup
1/2 teaspoon Worcestershire sauce
1 tablespoon pimiento
3 tablespoons sherry
Salt and pepper to taste
1/4 cup grated cheddar cheese

Melt butter in a skillet. Add onion, green pepper, celery, and mushrooms. Sauté 3 to 4 minutes. Add cubed turkey and ham; warm two more minutes. Add remaining ingredients, except cheese. Pour into a greased casserole dish and sprinkle cheese on top. Bake in a 350-degree oven for about 1 hour.

Turkey Tetrazzini

A delicious entrée with leftover turkey

2 tablespoons butter or margarine
1 medium onion, chopped
1 chicken bouillon cube
1 cup hot water
1 can (10-3/4-ounce) cream of mushroom soup
2 cups cooked turkey, cubed
1 teaspoon parsley flakes
Dash pepper
1 can (8-ounce) sliced mushrooms, drained
Cooked spaghetti

Melt butter in a Dutch oven or large skillet with high sides. Cook onion in butter until tender. Dissolve the chicken bouillon cube in 1 cup hot water. Add bouillon and soup to skillet. Stir mixture until smooth. Add cubed turkey, parsley, pepper and mushrooms. Cook over low heat, stirring occasionally, about 5 minutes. Stir in cooked spaghetti and cook until heated through.

Turkey Wild Rice Casserole

1/4 cup butter or margarine
1/2 cup onion, chopped
1/2 cup celery, sliced
1 small garlic clove, minced
1/4 cup quick-mixing flour
1 cup chicken broth
1-1/2 cups half-and-half
1 can (4-ounce) sliced mushrooms, drained, reserve liquid
3 cups cubed, cooked turkey
1 cup uncooked wild rice
1 cup frozen corn
Parsley flakes
Salt and pepper to taste
1/2 cup silvered almonds

Melt butter in a large skillet. Sauté onions, garlic and celery until tender. Sprinkle in flour and stir until well blended. Add chicken broth, half-and-half, and reserved liquid from mushrooms to flour mixture; blend until smooth. Cook until mixture has thickened, about 1 minute, stirring constantly. Add remaining ingredients, except almonds; mix well. Pour mixture into a greased casserole dish.

Bake at 350 degrees for 45 minutes. Remove from oven; sprinkle the top with almonds. Bake 10 to 15 minutes longer, or until wild rice has opened. If mixture becomes dry during baking, add more chicken broth.

Turkey Breast with Wild Rice Dressing

1 wild turkey breast, skin on, boned
1 can (14-1/2-ounce) chicken broth
1 cup uncooked wild rice
1/3 cup butter
1 cup celery, chopped
1 cup onion, finely chopped
1/2 pound seasoned pork sausage
1 can (8-ounce) mushrooms, drained
1/2 teaspoon salt
1/4 teaspoon pepper
1/4 to 1/2 teaspoon poultry seasoning
4 tablespoons butter, melted

Wash wild rice and drain. In a medium-sized pan, add chicken broth and wild rice. Cover, simmer for about 30 minutes or until rice has opened. Drain. Place cooked wild rice in a mixing bowl.

Melt butter in a skillet; sauté celery and onion. Add to wild rice. Lightly brown sausage in skillet. Remove sausage with slotted spoon to wild rice bowl. Add in remaining ingredients; mix well.

Lightly butter a small roasting pan or large casserole. Turn out wild rice mixture into roasting pan . Place breast on top of wild rice dressing. Brush turkey with melted butter. Cover and bake at 325 degrees for 1-1/2 hours to 2 hours or until breast is tender. Baste breast with melted butter frequently while baking.

Variations: 1) Stuff whole turkey with dressing mix. 2) Substitute pheasant for turkey.

Workday Turkey Casserole

Prepare ahead and pop in the oven when you get home

4 cups leftover turkey meat
1 10-ounce package frozen peas
1 can (10-3/4-ounce) cream of mushroom soup
1 can (12-ounce) evaporated milk
1/4 teaspoon poultry seasoning
Dash pepper
4 cups seasoned croutons
1 cup butter or margarine, melted

Mix meat, peas, mushroom soup, evaporated milk and seasoning. Turn into a greased casserole dish. Mix croutons with 1 cup melted butter; spread over turkey mixture. Cover and bake at 350 degrees for 35 to 40 minutes.

*Cube or dice leftover meat.
Freeze in 1 or 2 cup amounts;
label container, and use in recipes.*

SMALL

GAME

Small Game

Rabbit is delicious meat, comparable to chicken and just as easily varied with different combinations of herbs and spices. Individual spices and combinations, such as thyme, rosemary, paprika, marjoram, curry, clove – you get the picture – will work well.

As with most game, immediate field dressing is essential to the good, mild taste of the meat. Here is a "no fuss, no muss" tip to skin a rabbit or squirrel without dealing with the insides. Skin the animal while still warm. Cut the front and hind legs off; cut out the backstraps. You have the meat. Throw the remaining carcass away, insides intact. If this is done in the field, put the meat in a plastic zip-top bag to transport home on ice.

Any shot-damaged meat should be removed, prior to packaging or preparing the rabbit. If the animal is shot up, it may be soaked in brine for three to four hours. Make a brine of 1 tablespoon salt to each quart of water.

Rabbit is lean meat and may need additional fat, such as bacon, during dry-heat cooking. Older, tougher rabbits may need to be parboiled before using. However, a better way to tenderize and flavor rabbit is with a spicy marinade, such as Cooked Herb Marinade (see p. 241) or Game Wine Marinade (see p. 246).

Squirrel meat is tender and has a delicious flavor. Basically, the same cooking methods apply to squirrels and rabbits. Cooking small game is not terribly difficult and will add immensely to your menu options.

Brunswick Stew

3 squirrels, cut up
1/4 cup all-purpose flour
Salt and pepper
6 slices bacon cut into 1/2 inch pieces
5 cups water
1 can (28-ounce) whole tomatoes, not drained
1 medium onion, chopped
1 package (10-ounce) frozen lima beans
1-1/2 cups frozen whole-kernel corn
1 cup potatoes, diced
1/2 cup carrots, diced
1/2 cup celery, diced
1/2 cup cabbage, grated

In a plastic zip-top bag, combine flour, salt, and pepper. Add squirrel pieces and shake to coat. Fry bacon in a large kettle or Dutch oven over medium heat. Add squirrel pieces and brown on all sides. Add water, tomatoes, and onions in with browned squirrel. Bring to a boil. Reduce heat and cover. Simmer until squirrel pieces are tender, about 1-1/2 hours. Stir occasionally.

Remove meat from kettle and cool. When cool, pick meat from bones. Discard bones. Put meat back into kettle, along with remaining vegetables. Salt and pepper as needed. Cover and simmer until vegetables are tender, 25 to 35 minutes. Thicken stew by blending equal amounts of flour and cold water in small bowl. Slowly add to stew in small amounts, stirring constantly. Heat to a rolling boil. Cook over medium heat, stirring constantly, until thickened.

Burgundy Rabbit Casserole

1 rabbit, cut into serving pieces
1 cup burgundy wine
2 tablespoons red wine vinegar
2 tablespoons olive oil
1 medium onion, sliced
1 bay leaf, crushed
1/2 teaspoon dried thyme
1/2 teaspoon dried rosemary
1/8 teaspoon pepper
2 tablespoons olive oil
Salt and pepper

In a small bowl, combine wine, vinegar, 2 tablespoons olive oil, onion, bay leaf, thyme, rosemary, and pepper. Place rabbit pieces in a separate bowl and pour wine mixture over meat. Marinate in refrigerator for two hours. Remove rabbit pieces; dry with paper toweling. Save marinade.

Heat remaining 2 tablespoons olive oil in a skillet; brown rabbit pieces on all sides. Place browned meat in a casserole dish. Strain marinade; pour over meat. Add salt and pepper as desired. Cover casserole, bake at 325 degrees for 1-1/2 to 2 hours or until tender. Check casserole occasionally; add more wine if needed to keep meat covered with liquid.

Cheesy Rabbit Bake

1 rabbit (2-1/2 pounds) cut into serving pieces
1-1/2 cups cracker crumbs
1/2 cup vegetable oil
1 can (10-3/4-ounce) condensed cheddar cheese soup
3 tablespoons dry onion soup mix
1/2 cup milk

Coat rabbit pieces with cracker crumbs. In a large skillet, brown rabbit in hot oil. Remove rabbit to a baking dish. Discard oil. Combine soup, soup mix, and milk in a bowl; pour over rabbit. Sprinkle any remaining cracker crumbs over top. Bake at 350 degrees for 1 hour, or until rabbit is tender.

Creamed Squirrel on Rice

3 to 4 squirrels, cut up
Flour, all-purpose
2 tablespoons butter
1/8 cup olive oil
1 can (10-3/4-ounce) cream of mushroom soup
1 soup can milk
1 can (4-ounce) mushrooms, drained
3 tablespoons sherry
1/2 teaspoon poultry seasoning
1 medium onion, chopped
Steamed rice

Coat squirrel pieces in flour. Heat butter and olive oil in medium skillet. Fry meat until lightly browned. Remove squirrel from skillet. Combine cream of mushroom soup with one soup can of milk; pour into skillet. Stir, loosening browned particles. Add mushrooms, onions, poultry seasoning, and stir in sherry. Return squirrel to skillet; season with salt and pepper. Cover and simmer, 1 to 1-1/2 hours or until meat is tender, turning often. Adjust seasonings. Serve over steamed rice.

Variation: Use cream of celery soup instead of cream of mushroom soup.

Creamy Rabbit Casserole

Delicious served with wild rice or over buttered noodles

2 rabbits, cut into serving pieces
5 tablespoons all-purpose flour
5 tablespoons butter
1 large onion, chopped
1/2 to 1 cup celery, chopped
6 whole allspice
2 bay leaves, crushed
1/4 cup cider vinegar
2 cups chicken broth
1/2 cup half-and-half
1-1/2 tablespoons plum or apple butter
Salt and pepper

Dredge rabbit pieces in 3 tablespoons of flour seasoned with salt and pepper. Heat 3 tablespoons of butter in a heavy skillet; brown rabbit pieces on all sides. Transfer rabbit to heavy casserole or Dutch oven.

Sauté onion in skillet until tender. Add to casserole. Place celery, allspice, bay leaves, and vinegar in casserole. Pour in enough broth to barely cover rabbit. Bring mixture to a boil. Cover and reduce heat to simmer. Simmer until rabbit is tender, about 1 hour.

Melt remaining 2 tablespoons butter in a small saucepan, add 2 tablespoons flour. Stir until lightly browned. Using a wire whisk, stir flour mixture into casserole. Cook for 3 minutes. Season to taste. Stir in half-and-half, plum or apple butter. Heat until plum or apple butter is blended.

Crock-Pot Squirrel or Rabbit

3 to 6 dressed squirrels, cut into pieces
2 carrots, peeled and sliced
1/4 cup soy sauce
1/4 cup water
1/4 cup firmly packed brown sugar
3 tablespoons lemon juice
1/4 teaspoon garlic powder
1/4 teaspoon ground ginger
2 tablespoons quick-mixing flour
3 tablespoons cold water

Place squirrel pieces and carrots in Crock-Pot. Mix remaining ingredients in a small bowl; pour over meat. Cover and cook on low heat for 7 to 8 hours. To thicken gravy, mix flour with cold water. Stir liquid into Crock-Pot. Cook on high until thickened, stirring frequently.

Curry Rabbit in Cream Sauce

1 rabbit, cut into serving pieces
1 clove garlic, halved
1 cup flour, all-purpose
2 tablespoons dry mustard
1 teaspoon curry powder
1 teaspoon powdered thyme
2 teaspoons salt
1/2 teaspoon pepper
2 tablespoons vegetable oil
1 cup half-and-half

Rub rabbit with cut side of garlic. In a plastic zip-top bag, combine flour, mustard, curry powder, thyme, salt, and pepper. Shake rabbit pieces in flour mixture. Remove, shake off excess. Set aside.

Heat oil in a skillet; brown rabbit until golden brown on all sides. Remove rabbit pieces; add half-and-half, stir to blend with pan juices. Reduce heat to simmer. Return rabbit to pan. Cover and simmer 1 hour or until tender.

Effortless Baked Squirrel

4 squirrels, cut into serving-sized pieces
1/2 cup flour, all-purpose
Salt and pepper
3 tablespoons olive oil
3 tablespoons onion, chopped
1 can (14-1/2-ounce) beef or chicken broth
Clove of garlic, minced
1 whole bay leaf
2 tablespoons fresh parsley, chopped
1/4 cup Worcestershire sauce

Place flour, salt, and pepper in a plastic zip-top bag. Place meat in bag; shake to coat. Heat olive oil in a medium skillet; brown squirrel on all sides. Remove meat with a slotted spoon and place in a roasting pan. Add broth and remaining ingredients. Bake at 325 degrees for 1-1/2 hours or until tender.

Fricasseed Squirrel

4 to 5 squirrels, cut into pieces
1 cup flour, all-purpose
Salt and pepper
5 slices of bacon, diced
1 medium onion, sliced
1-1/2 teaspoons fresh lemon juice
2/3 cup beef or chicken broth

Mix flour, salt and pepper together. Coat squirrel pieces in flour mixture. In a heavy skillet fry bacon until browned. Add squirrel and lightly brown. Add remaining ingredients to skillet. Cover; simmer for about 1 hour or until meat is tender. Add more broth during cooking time, if it becomes dry.

Garlic-Honey Marinated Rabbit

2 rabbits (3 to 3-1/2 pounds) dressed, cut into serving pieces
3/4 cup lemon juice
3/4 cup honey
6 tablespoons soy sauce
3 tablespoons dry sherry
6 garlic cloves, minced

Combine lemon juice, honey, soy sauce, sherry, and cloves in a large shallow bowl; add rabbit pieces. Cover, refrigerate for 8 hours. Turn rabbit occasionally.

Remove rabbit; drain off pieces. Discard marinade. Arrange rabbit in a 9- by 13-inch baking pan. Cover; bake at 325 degrees for 1 to 1-1/2 hours or until rabbit is tender.

Quick Rabbit Barbecue

Excellent recipe to use with older, tougher rabbit meat –use pressure cooker to cook rabbit

2 rabbits, dressed and cut into quarters
3/4 cups water
2 tablespoons butter
1/2 cup onions, chopped
1/4 cup green pepper, diced
1/4 cup celery, diced
1 tablespoon sugar
1 tablespoon salt
1/4 teaspoon pepper
1 cup tomato soup or puree
1 tablespoon vinegar
1/4 cup ketchup
Dash or two hot sauce

For a 4-quart pressure cooker, add 3/4 cup water and rabbit quarters. Set control at 10 pounds of pressure. After control jiggles, cook 18 to 20 minutes. Cool pan normally for 5 minutes, then place under faucet. Remove cover. Remove meat from bone and cut into small pieces.

Melt butter in a skillet. Sauté onions, green pepper, and celery until tender. Remove from heat; stir in rabbit meat and remainder of ingredients. Return to heat, simmer at least 1/2 hour, adding water if necessary. Serve on toast or toasted buns. Makes about one quart.

Note*:* Follow manufacturer's instructions regarding pressure cooker.

Tip: Prepare recipe ahead of time, freeze and use later.

Rabbit Hasenpfeffer

2 rabbits, cut into serving pieces
3 cups water
3 cups cider vinegar
1/2 cup brown sugar
1 large onion, sliced
2 teaspoons salt
10 whole black peppercorns
1 clove garlic, minced fine
1 bay leaf, crushed
2 teaspoons pickling spices
1/4 cup all-purpose flour
3 tablespoons butter

Place pieces in a non-metallic bowl or plastic zip-top bag. Mix the next 9 ingredients and pour over rabbit. Cover bowl or seal bag; refrigerate for two days. During this time, turn pieces so they are covered by the marinade.

Drain rabbit pieces, reserve marinade. Pat pieces dry. Rub with flour. Heat butter in a heavy skillet, brown rabbit pieces on all sides. Transfer to a casserole dish. Heat reserved marinade in a saucepan, bringing to a boil. Boil for several minutes. Pour enough of the marinade in casserole to cover rabbit pieces halfway. Cover and bake at 350 degrees about 1 hour or until meat is tender.

Rabbit Jumped into the Frying Pan

1 rabbit, cut into serving pieces
Salt and pepper
1/8 teaspoon crushed oregano
1 egg
2 tablespoons milk
1/4 cup all-purpose flour
1/2 cup fine dry bread crumbs
1/2 cup vegetable oil

Mix salt, pepper, and oregano together in a bowl; rub each rabbit piece with seasonings. Combine milk and egg; beat lightly. Dip seasoned rabbit in flour, then in egg mixture, and then into the bread crumbs. Heat oil in a frying pan; brown rabbit on all sides. Reduce heat. Cook 20 to 30 minutes longer or until tender. Drain on paper toweling.

Rabbit Stew and Potato Dumplings

1 rabbit, dressed, cut into serving pieces
1 large onion, chopped
2 whole bay leaves
1/2 teaspoon garlic black pepper seasoning
1/2 teaspoon salt
1 teaspoon dried tarragon
1 teaspoon dried thyme
Water
4 large carrots, peeled, chunked
4 medium potatoes, peeled, chunked
1 recipe Potato Dumplings (See p. 235)

Place rabbit pieces in a large kettle or Dutch oven. Add onion, bay leaves, garlic pepper seasoning, salt, tarragon, and thyme. Pour in water to cover ingredients. Cover; cook over medium-low heat 1-1/2 hours. Add carrots and potatoes. Cover; increase heat to medium. Bring to a rolling boil. While vegetables are cooking, prepare Potato Dumpling recipe. Drop dumplings, one at a time into gently boiling mixture. Cover; reduce heat to simmer. Stir occasionally; cook 15 minutes or until vegetables are tender and dumplings cooked.

Smothered Wild Rice & Fried Squirrel

2 squirrels, cut into serving pieces
Flour, all-purpose
Salt and pepper
1/2 cup butter or margarine
1 can (10-3/4-ounce) cream of chicken soup
1/2 cup water
4 cups cooked wild rice

Either parboil or pressure cook squirrel until almost tender. Remove from pan. Combine flour, salt, and pepper; coat meat with flour. Melt butter in a skillet; add meat and brown on all sides. Remove; set aside.

Combine soup, water, and wild rice in skillet. Stir, loosening particles from bottom of skillet. Place mixture in a lightly buttered baking dish. Season with salt and pepper to taste. Arrange fried squirrel pieces on top. Cover; bake at 325 degrees for about 30 minutes until mixture is hot.

Variation: Follow recipe above, substituting rabbit or venison. With venison, omit parboiling. Cube meat into 1 inch cubes, brown in skillet. Proceed as directed above.

Spicy Rabbit with Bacon Gravy

1 rabbit, dressed, cut into serving pieces
1/2 cup all-purpose flour
1/2 teaspoon salt
1/4 teaspoon pepper
1/2 pound bacon, chopped
1 cup sweet onions, chopped
1 clove garlic, chopped
1 cup red wine
1 cup water
1 tablespoon instant chicken bouillon granules
2 tablespoons currant jelly
1/4 teaspoon dried rosemary
1/8 teaspoon dried thyme
1 whole bay leaf
3 tablespoons reserved flour
2 tablespoons water

Combine flour, salt, and pepper in a plastic zip-top bag. Shake all rabbit pieces in flour to coat. Remove and set aside. Reserve flour mixture for use later.

In a cast iron or large skillet over medium heat, fry bacon until crisp. Remove bacon with slotted spoon; drain, crumble, and set aside. Brown all rabbit pieces in hot bacon drippings. Remove as pieces brown to a container. Drain off all but 2 tablespoons of drippings from skillet. Fry onions and garlic in skillet until tender. Stir in wine, water, bouillon granules, jelly, rosemary, thyme and bay leaf. Add rabbit back into skillet. Heat to boiling; reduce heat to simmer, and cover. Simmer for 1-1/2 hours or until rabbit is tender. Remove and discard bay leaf. Remove rabbit with a slotted spoon to a covered serving dish. Keep warm. Blend 3 tablespoons reserved flour and water until smooth. Gradually pour into liquid stirring constantly until desired thickness. Add crumbled bacon to gravy. Serve gravy with rabbit.

Squirrel or Rabbit Stew

3 squirrels or 1 rabbit cut into serving pieces
1 can (10-3/4-ounce) condensed cream of mushroom soup
1 can (10-3/4-ounce) condensed cream of potato soup
1 cup milk
1 can (15-ounce) whole kernel corn, undrained
1 cup frozen peas
Salt and pepper
1/2 teaspoon crushed red pepper
1-1/2 pounds fresh mushrooms, sliced
3 tablespoons butter
3 tablespoons all-purpose flour
3 tablespoons cold water

Soak cleaned squirrels or rabbit in salt water for one hour. Drain, discarding liquid. Put pieces into a large kettle with enough water to cover. Parboil for 15 to 20 minutes. Remove meat to a dish. When meat has cooled enough to handle, clean meat from bones. Cut into bite-size pieces. Discard bones and water.

In the large kettle, add both soups, milk, corn, peas, red pepper, and meat. Salt and pepper to taste. Bring to a boil; reduce heat, cover and simmer. While stew simmers, sauté mushrooms in butter. Add mushrooms to stew pot. Continue simmering for 10 minutes. If stew is thinner than desired, blend flour and water in a small bowl. Add to stew, stirring constantly. Heat to boiling. Cook over medium heat, stirring constantly, until thickened.

Stew Pot Rabbit

1 rabbit, cut up
2 large onions, chopped
1 whole bay leaf
1-1/2 cups diced celery
4-1/2 teaspoon salt
1/8 teaspoon pepper
2 quarts boiling water
2 cups carrots, peeled and diced
2 cups potatoes, peeled and diced
1/2 pound fresh mushrooms, sliced
1/4 teaspoon fresh rosemary, snipped
1/2 cup all-purpose flour
3/4 cup cold water
1 tablespoon fresh parsley, snipped
Dash or two liquid hot pepper seasoning

Wash and dry rabbit pieces. Place in kettle with onions, bay leaf, celery, salt, pepper, and water. Cover and simmer for 2 hours or until rabbit is nearly tender. Add carrots, potatoes, mushrooms, and rosemary. Cover; continue to simmer 30 minutes longer or until all is tender. Discard bay leaf. Blend flour with water. Stir into stew. Cook until thickened, stirring frequently. Add parsley and hot pepper seasoning.

Sweet-Sour Rabbit

2 to 3 pounds rabbit, cut into serving pieces
1/4 cup all-purpose flour
Salt and pepper
2 tablespoons vegetable oil
1 cup pineapple juice
1/4 cup vinegar
1-1/2 cup pineapple pieces, drained
1 green pepper, seeded, cut into thin strips
1-1/2 tablespoons cornstarch
1/8 to 1/4 cup sugar (depending on how sweet/sour sauce is)
1/2 cup water

Combine flour, salt and pepper in a shallow bowl. Roll rabbit pieces in flour mixture. Heat oil in a heavy skillet over moderate heat. Brown rabbit on all sides. Add pineapple juice, vinegar and salt. Reduce heat to simmer. Cover, cook for 40 minutes or until meat is tender. Add pineapple pieces and green pepper; cook until green pepper is tender. Mix cornstarch and sugar; stir in water. Gradually stir cornstarch mixture into liquid in skillet. Stir constantly until slightly thickened. Serve over white rice.

Wood-Lot Squirrel

A "honey" of a dish

2 squirrels, cut into serving pieces
Water
1 teaspoon salt
1/2 cup all-purpose flour
1/4 teaspoon pepper
1/2 cup olive oil
1 cup chicken broth
3 Granny Smith apples, peeled and sliced thick
4 tablespoons honey
4 tablespoons brown sugar

Place squirrel pieces in a kettle or Dutch oven. Add salt and just enough water to cover squirrel. Bring to a boil; cover and cook until squirrel is tender. Remove from water. Dry squirrel pieces on paper toweling. Discard water. Combine flour and pepper in shallow dish. Coat squirrel with mixture. Set aside.

Heat oil in a skillet over medium-high heat. Fry squirrel on all sides. When browned, remove to a baking pan; add chicken broth. Place apples on top of squirrel pieces. Mix together honey and brown sugar; spread over top. Bake for 30 minutes at 350 degrees, or until apples are tender.

DUCKS
&
GEESE

After the Duck and Goose Hunt

In the early years of our country, it is reported that the skies would be filled from horizon to horizon with flocks upon flocks of ducks and geese. There were so many it would look like huge dark clouds undulating across the heavens, almost blocking the sun. Early duck and goose hunters had no trouble bagging their limits. Old timers' stories of the good-old days usually included some mention of the hearty meals of their harvest that put the final touch on a grand day of hunting. Today, throughout the country, hunting waterfowl in the crisp days of autumn is still a favorite sport of many.

To ensure your birds will keep their best flavor between the hunting grounds and home, keep the birds cool. If the weather isn't cold, take along a cooler to transport the birds. Field dress the birds and cool the carcasses quickly to retain flavor and maintain quality. Wipe the cavity with paper toweling or a clean cloth and keep them cool until you reach home. Place them individually in plastic bags and put them on ice quickly. Handle geese in the same manner as ducks.

Wild game connoisseurs prefer ducks and geese be plucked rather than skinned, because the skin helps retain flavor and moisture during cooking. However, for quick, easy cleaning, skinning is a faster method. To skin a bird, it is easier to proceed when the bird is still warm. Make a small incision near where the leg meets the body, insert your fingers and pull the skin away from the flesh. Breasting out the bird, that is simply removing the breast meat is another option. While the bird is warm, pull the skin away from the breast and use a sharp knife to fillet the meat away from bone by cutting straight down along the breast bone. If there are any bloody spots on the bird, these can be eliminated by cutting them out or rinsing them with cold water. Always be on the lookout for birdshot. The entry wounds are fairly easy to see once the bird is skinned. Try to remove as many of the pellets as possible before cooking the bird.

Freeze birds if they are not being prepared right away. Do not freeze birds that have not been plucked and cleaned first. After cleaning the birds, wrap with a moisture- and vapor-proof material. Label the package, including the date, and freeze it immediately. Thaw out packaged birds in the refrigerator for about 12 hours. The length of time ducks and geese can be frozen is about six months.

Ducks and geese may be baked, barbecued, breaded, broiled, grilled, fried, combined in casseroles, and made into chop suey, Creole, gumbos and gravies. Wild duck meat is rich, dark meat and is somewhat more dry than domestic duck. If the birds have been skinned, some type of moisture needs to be added during cooking. One method is to place strips of bacon over the breast of a skinned bird and then roast in a covered pan. When roasting or broiling ducks, use a rack in the bottom of the pan. This keeps the birds away from the grease in the bottom of the pan. Do not use this grease for basting, because it has an unpleasant flavor.

Well-fed birds with the skin left on may be rendered of excess fat prior to being prepared in a recipe. Rendering can be done before freezing the bird, or before meal preparation. Directions follow.

Rendering Fowl

To render, place a cleaned duck or goose on a rack in the bottom of a roaster. Cover the roaster and place in an oven set at 400 to 425 degrees. Monitor closely, until all or most of the fat runs off the bird. The bird **should not be turning brown** during this process. You are not cooking the bird at this time; just rendering off the fat. Rendering time varies from 10 minutes to 1 hour, depending on the type of the bird. It is important to remove the bird before it is browned. Use paper towels to wipe excess fat off the outside and from the cavity. It is now ready for your favorite recipe.

The age of the bird determines the cooking method. Young birds have lighter legs, soft breastbones, and flexible beaks. Dry cooking methods, such as frying, are appropriate for young birds. Older birds have darker, hard-skinned legs, brittle breastbones, and inflexible beaks. Moist cooking methods, such as stewing or braising, are appropriate for these older birds.

Now, let's get cooking!

Ducks vary in size, therefore, cooking times are approximate.

Crock-Pot Duck Fillets Italiano

1 package (8-ounce) frozen peas
1 cup carrots, chopped
1 large onion, chopped
1/3 cup water
1 can (8-ounce) tomato sauce
1/2 cup dry red wine
1 teaspoon garlic powder
1/2 teaspoon thyme
1/8 teaspoon ground cloves
2 whole bay leaves
1 can (15-ounce) navy beans, drained
4 duck breast fillets
1 package (8-ounce) spicy Italian sausage, sliced

Bring peas, carrots, onion, and water to a boil in saucepan; reduce heat. Simmer, covered, for 5 minutes. Place in a 4-quart crock-pot. Stir in tomato sauce, wine, seasonings, and beans. Lay duck fillets and sausage on top of bean mixture. Cook on low for 8 hours or on high for 6 hours or until duck fillets are tender. Discard bay leaves before serving.

Currant Duck Breasts

4 mallard duck breasts, skin off, halved
4 tablespoons butter or margarine
1/3 cup brandy
1/3 cup sherry
1/4 cup currant jelly
1 tablespoon Worcestershire sauce
2 teaspoons cornstarch
2 tablespoons cold water
3 cups cooked wild rice

Melt butter in a skillet; stir in brandy, sherry, jelly, and Worcestershire sauce. Bring mixture to a boil; add breasts to skillet. Cover; reduce heat and simmer 30 minutes, or until meat is tender. Turn breasts several times during cooking. Dish hot wild rice in a large casserole and lay duck breasts on top. Cover and keep warm.

Blend cornstarch and water; slowly stir into liquid in skillet. Cook over low heat, stirring until sauce thickens. Pour sauce over duck breasts and serve.

Delectable Roast Goose with Stuffing

1 (6 pound) goose, dressed
Salt and pepper
1/2 pound chicken livers
1 goose liver and heart
2 cups chicken broth
1/2 pound sausage meat
1 medium Granny Smith apple, cored, diced
1/4 cup fresh mushrooms, chopped
1 cup soft bread crumbs
1/2 teaspoon dried rosemary
1/4 teaspoon dried tarragon
3 to 4 slices bacon
1 cup dry white wine
1 cup orange juice
1 tablespoon grated orange rind
1 tablespoon lemon juice
1/2 cup water
1 cup heavy cream
2 tablespoons currant jelly

Season goose inside and outside with salt and pepper. Place chicken livers, goose liver and heart, and broth in small saucepan. Simmer until livers are tender. Drain; discard liquid. Chop livers and heart in very fine pieces. Set aside.

In a skillet, fry the sausage meat until no longer pink. Remove meat with a slotted spoon to a large bowl. Discard drippings. Combine liver mixture, sausage, apples, mushrooms, bread crumbs, rosemary, and tarragon. Combine white wine, orange rind, and lemon juice in a small bowl. Stuff the goose with bread mixture. Close and truss goose. Place bird on a rack in a roasting pan. Lay strips of bacon across breast. Roast, uncovered, at 450 degrees for 15 minutes. Reduce heat to 350 degrees. Continue to roast about 2 hours longer, or until tender. Baste frequently with wine mixture.

Remove bird to a warm platter. Drain excess grease from drippings. Discard grease. Return remaining drippings to roasting pan; add water. Have heat under roasting pan on low. Stir to loosen any remaining browned bits. Slowly stir in cream and then jelly. Heat until hot; do not boil. Serve sauce separately with goose and dressing.

Duck & Wild Rice En Casserole

2 ducks, dressed and halved
1 can (8-ounce) sliced mushrooms, drained,
1/2 cup celery, chopped
1/2 cup onion, chopped
1 tablespoon Worcestershire sauce
1/2 teaspoon black pepper
1 cup uncooked wild rice
1 can (14-1/2 ounces) chicken broth
2 cans (10-3/4 ounces) cream of mushroom soup
2 whole bay leaves

In a medium-sized bowl, mix together chicken broth and mushroom soup. Add sliced mushrooms, celery, onion, Worcestershire sauce, and black pepper. Stir to combine all ingredients. Place wild rice in a large casserole dish or small roasting pan. Pour broth and soup mixture over wild rice; mix well Add bay leaves.

Lay duck pieces on top of wild rice mixture, lightly pressing pieces into wild rice. Cover; bake at 325 degrees for 2 hours, until rice and meat are tender. If mixture becomes dry during baking, add more chicken broth. Remove bay leaves before serving. Serve with Sweet and Tangy Carrots. (see p. 237)

Flavorful Wild Duck

1 duck, cleaned and quartered
Salt and pepper
1/4 cup bacon drippings or vegetable oil
1 cup beef broth
1 cup orange juice
3 tablespoons grated orange rind
1/2 cup dry vermouth
1/3 cup light brown sugar
Cornstarch

Season duck quarters with salt and pepper; brown in bacon drippings in a heavy skillet. Add the beef broth. Cover, reduce heat and simmer for 1 hour.

In a small bowl, mix orange juice, orange rind, vermouth, and brown sugar. Add to skillet with the duck. Cover and continue to simmer until duck is tender, approximately 30 minutes. Remove duck pieces to a warm platter and keep warm.

For each cup liquid left in the skillet, add 1-1/2 tablespoons cornstarch mixed with three tablespoons water. Bring to a boil, stirring frequently. Reduce heat, continue to stir until mixture thickens and becomes translucent. Season to taste with salt and pepper. Serve sauce in a sauce dish. Garnish duck with orange slices and sprigs of parsley.

Flyway Fried Duck

4 duck breast fillets, skin off
1 egg
2 tablespoons milk
3/4 cup seasoned dry bread crumbs
1/4 teaspoon poultry seasoning
Bacon drippings

Pound duck fillets to 1/4 inch thickness with a meat mallet. In a shallow bowl, beat egg and milk until foamy. Combine bread crumbs and seasoning in another shallow bowl. Dip duck fillets in egg, then in the bread crumbs. Heat bacon drippings in a skillet over medium heat; sauté fillets until browned and cooked to desired degree of doneness.

Fried Goose Breast

2 goose breast halves
1/3 cup all-purpose flour
Salt and pepper
2 tablespoons olive oil
1 tablespoon butter
2 medium onions, sliced

Slice breasts into 1/4 to 1/2 inch slices. Salt and pepper goose slices; dredge in flour. Heat oil and butter in skillet; sauté onion until tender. Remove and set aside. In same skillet, brown goose slices well on both sides. Continue to cook until meat is tender. Serve slices with onions spooned over top.

Goose Cacciatore

Mama mia, what a tasty dish. And so easy too, when you use an electric skillet.

2 goose breasts, skin off, filleted
3 to 4 tablespoons quick-mixing flour
1/4 cup olive oil
2 cloves garlic, minced
1/2 cup Italian tomato paste
1/2 cup Chardonnay wine
1 teaspoon salt
1/4 teaspoon pepper
3/4 cup chicken broth
1 bay leaf, crushed
1/8 teaspoon thyme
1/8 teaspoon marjoram
1/2 teaspoon basil leaves
1/2 cup onions, chopped
1 can (8 ounces) sliced mushrooms, drained
1/4 cup brandy

Slice goose fillets in 1/4-inch thick slices. Coat both sides of slices with flour. Heat olive oil in a skillet. Add in garlic and goose slices; sauté for 5 minutes on each side. In a bowl, combine remaining ingredients; mix well. Pour mixture over goose and cover. Simmer for about 1 hour or until meat is tender. Serve over hot, cooked vermicelli along with thick slices of toasted garlic bread.

Honey-Glazed Quacker

1 large or 2 small ducks, dressed, skin on
1 teaspoon seasoned salt
1 teaspoon poultry seasoning
1/2 cup honey
1/3 cup orange-flavored liqueur or orange juice
1-1/2 teaspoons dry mustard

In a bowl, combine seasoned salt and poultry seasoning. Rub cavity and skin with seasoning mixture. Place duck(s) on a rack in a baking pan or small roaster. Bake in a 375-degree oven for 1 hour.

Blend honey, liqueur, and mustard in a bowl. Drain off accumulated grease from pan; discard. Brush duck with honey mixture; continue to bake 45 to 60 minutes longer, until duck is golden brown and meat is tender. Periodically, brush remaining glaze over duck during baking.

Marinated Savory Duck

2 ducks, skin off, cut into serving pieces
1/4 cup all-purpose flour
1/2 teaspoon salt
1/4 teaspoon coarse ground pepper
2 tablespoons butter
1 tablespoon olive oil
Water
1 can (8-ounce) sliced mushrooms, drained
Quick-mixing flour

Marinade:

1 cup red wine
2 crushed peppercorns
2 teaspoons salt
1/4 teaspoon ground thyme
1/2 teaspoon dry parsley
1 crushed bay leaf
1 large onion, chopped

Mix all marinade ingredients in a plastic zip-top bag or non-metallic bowl. Place duck pieces in bag or bowl; cover with marinade. Cover bowl; refrigerate overnight. When ready to use, remove duck pieces; pat dry. Strain and save marinade. Discard remainder.

Combine flour, salt and pepper in a shallow bowl. Coat duck with flour. Shake off excess. In an electric skillet or large frying pan, melt butter; add oil. Brown duck on all sides. Add reserved marinade and enough water to cover meat. Add mushrooms. Cover, simmer for 1 to 1-1/2 hours, or until duck is tender. Remove duck to a serving dish and keep warm.

Thicken pan liquid by shaking in a little quick-mixing flour. Stir until desired consistency. Add salt and pepper to taste. Serve with mashed potatoes, white rice or wild rice.

Nutty Apple Mallard

2 mallards or 1 goose, dressed, skin on
8 tablespoons butter or margarine, divided
2 large ribs celery, sliced thin
1 large onion, diced
3 cups dry bread crumbs
2/3 cup chopped walnuts or pecans
1 apple, cored, diced
1 teaspoon salt
1/2 teaspoon pepper
1/2 teaspoon dried thyme
1 to 1-1/2 cups chicken broth
2 teaspoons soy sauce

Melt 4 tablespoons butter in a skillet; sauté celery and onion until tender. In a bowl, combine bread crumbs, walnuts, apple, celery, onion, salt, pepper, and thyme. Add enough broth to stuffing, moisten as desired. Stuff cavity with mixture. Place ducks breast side up on rack in baking pan or roaster. Add 1/2 cup water to bottom of pan. Cover; bake at 350 degrees for 1 hour.

Melt remaining butter in small saucepan; add soy sauce. Stir to blend. Uncover ducks; baste with butter mixture. Continue to bake uncovered, 45 to 60 minutes, or until tender. Baste frequently with butter mixture.

Parmesan Breaded Duck Cutlets

2 duck breasts, skin off, boned, sliced thin
1/4 cup Parmesan cheese
3/4 cup canned seasoned bread crumbs
1 beaten egg
2 teaspoons milk
2 tablespoons olive oil

In a small bowl, mix Parmesan cheese and seasoned bread crumbs. In separate small bowl, beat egg and milk. Dip cutlets in egg mixture, and then roll in Parmesan cheese mixture. Heat oil in a heavy skillet. When hot, fry breast slices quickly. Serve hot with Cranberry Ketchup (See p. 242) on the side.

Roast Duck with Apricot Sauce

3 ducks, skin on
1 teaspoon salt
Fresh ground black pepper
Celery leaves, coarsely chopped
1 cup butter or margarine, melted, divided
1/2 cup dry red wine
Apricot Sauce

Rub cavity of each duck with salt and pepper. Fill cavity with celery leaves. Place ducks in roasting pan, breast side up. Brush skin with 1/2 cup of the butter. Roast for 30 minutes in a 450-degree oven. Baste ducks every 5 minutes with 1/2 cup of red wine and remaining 1/2 cup butter. Remove ducks from pan. Carve into serving pieces, cover and keep warm. Save pan juices to add to apricot sauce.

Apricot Sauce:

2-1/2 cups canned peeled apricots, drained
1 teaspoon grated orange rind
2 cups dry red wine
6 tablespoons butter or margarine
Fresh ground black pepper
Pan juices from roasted duck

Press apricots through a coarse sieve or mash with a fork. Combine apricots, orange rind, wine, butter and pepper in a saucepan. Add in pan juices from roasted duck. Cook over medium heat for 5 minutes. Reduce heat and simmer for 5 minutes, stirring constantly, until sauce has slightly thickened. Pour over duck and serve immediately.

Roast Duck with Apricot Stuffing

2 ducks, skin on
1 stick butter
3/4 cup celery, chopped
1 medium onion, diced
2 cups dry bread crumbs
1/2 cup dried apricots cut up
1/2 cup walnuts or pecans, chopped
1/2 teaspoon thyme
Salt and pepper
1 cup chicken broth

To make stuffing, melt 4 tablespoons butter in skillet. Sauté celery and onions until almost tender. In a mixing bowl add bread crumbs, celery and onions, apricots, walnuts, thyme, salt and pepper. Stir in enough chicken broth to create desired consistency.

Melt remaining butter in a saucepan. Rub ducks inside and out with 2 teaspoons melted margarine, salt and pepper. Stuff ducks and wrap them in foil. Place foil wrapped ducks in a shallow baking pan; bake at 325 degrees for 1-1/2 hours. Open foil; baste with remaining melted butter. Keep unwrapped; continue to bake another 1/2 hour or until ducks become golden brown and tender.

Roast Duck with Kraut Stuffing

2 ducks, skin on
1 can (29-ounce) sauerkraut, drained
1 apple, pared and chopped
1/2 cup celery, finely chopped
2 tablespoons minced onion
Salt and pepper
2 strips bacon

Combine sauerkraut, celery, onion, and apple in a bowl. Lightly salt and pepper cavities of birds. Stuff sauerkraut mixture into cavities. Close cavity with skewers, if possible. Lay a bacon strip across each breast. Spread some of the sauerkraut over top of breasts. Roast at 325 degrees for 1-1/2 to 2 hours, or until tender. Remove stuffing and place in a serving bowl.

Roast Duck with Madeira Sauce

2 ducks, skin on
3 tablespoons butter or margarine
2 carrots, peeled, diced fine
2 ribs celery, chopped fine
1 can (2.25 ounces) sliced ripe olives, chopped
2 onions, coarsely chopped
1/4 cup vegetable oil
Salt and pepper
1/2 cup chicken broth
1/2 cup Madeira wine
2 tablespoons cornstarch
2 tablespoons cold water

Melt butter in a skillet. Add carrots, celery, and olives; cook for 5 minutes. Spread mixture in a small roasting pan; sprinkle with salt and pepper. Arrange ducks on top of mixture breast side up. Place an equal amount of onion in each cavity. Brush breasts with vegetable oil. Salt and pepper. Pour chicken broth and wine in bottom of pan. Roast in a 350-degree oven for 1-1/2 to 2 hours, or until tender.

Place ducks on a serving platter and keep hot. Discard stuffing. Strain pan juices into a small saucepan. Discard remainder. Blend cornstarch and water in a small bowl. Stir into pan juices. Heat to boiling stirring constantly. Lower heat to medium-high. Cook, stirring constantly until mixture is translucent. Serve sauce in a gravy boat.

When serving duck or goose, as a reminder, warn about possible pellets of shot in the meat.

Saucy Duck Breasts with Wild Rice

3 cups cooked wild rice
4 duck breast halves, boned, skin off
8 tablespoons butter or margarine
1/3 cup brandy
1/3 cup sherry
1-1/2 tablespoons grape jelly
1 tablespoon Worcestershire sauce
2 teaspoons cornstarch
2 tablespoons water
Dash of pepper

Melt butter in a skillet; add brandy, sherry, grape jelly and Worcestershire sauce. Stir mixture to dissolve grape jelly. Bring to a gentle boil. Add duck breasts; cover skillet. Reduce heat and simmer for 20 minutes, turning breast over after first 10 minutes. When tender, remove breasts to a warm serving dish. Cover and keep warm.

Blend cornstarch and water in a small bowl. Add a small amount hot liquid from the skillet to cornstarch mixture and stir. Over low heat, slowly pour cornstarch mixture into skillet. Stir until sauce thickens and becomes translucent.

To serve, place hot, cooked wild rice on individual plates. Slice each breast in thin slices and place meat fan-like on top of rice. Spoon sauce over breasts.

Sautéed Cutlets of Goose

1 goose, skin off, breasted, boned
1 cup all-purpose flour
2 eggs
3 tablespoons milk
2 cups packaged dry seasoned bread crumbs
1 teaspoon dried parsley
4 to 6 tablespoons butter or margarine
1 recipe Basic White Sauce (see p. 239)
3 tablespoons green onions with tops, minced fine

Cut goose breast into 1/2-inch thick cutlet across the grain. Place cutlet between two sheets of heavy plastic wrap. Pound gently to 1/4-inch thickness with flat side of meat mallet or edge of saucer. Repeat with remaining cutlets.

In a bowl, beat eggs and milk until frothy. Place flour and bread crumbs, each in a separate shallow bowl. Dust cutlets with flour; dip in egg and then coat with bread crumbs. In a medium skillet, melt 4 tablespoons butter over medium heat. Add half goose cutlets. Cook until golden brown and cooked through, turning once. Remove to baking pan; keep warm in 175-degree oven. If necessary, add remaining butter to skillet. Cook remaining cutlets.

Prepare white sauce; add green onions. Cook over low heat 3 to 5 minutes until onions are tender; stir frequently. Serve sauce over cutlets.

Savory Honker Stew

1 goose, boned, cubed
1/2 cup all-purpose flour
1/2 teaspoon salt
1/4 teaspoon pepper
3 tablespoons olive oil
1 envelope dried onion soup mix
1 large onion, chopped
1 cup frozen green beans
3 carrots, peeled and chunked
2 ribs celery, sliced
1 can (8 ounces) sliced mushrooms, undrained
1/2 teaspoon dried basil
1/2 teaspoon tarragon
1/2 teaspoon oregano
1 garlic clove, minced fine
1 whole bay leaf
2 to 3 cups beef broth
4 medium potatoes, peeled and chunked
Salt and pepper

In a plastic zip-top bag, add flour, salt and pepper; mix. Coat goose cubes in flour. Heat oil in skillet over moderate-high heat; brown goose meat on all sides. Place in a roaster. Add remaining ingredients, except potatoes. Salt and pepper to taste. Cover; bake at 325 degrees for 2 hours. Reduce temperature to 275 degrees. Add potatoes. Leave uncovered, bake for 1 hour longer, or until goose is tender. Thicken juice if desired with all-purpose flour.

Tip: Remove any fat, muscle and stringy tissue before cubing meat.

Southwestern Duck

2 ducks, skin on
1 cup celery, diced
1 cup onions, minced
1 cup golden raisins
1 cup pecans or walnuts, coarsely chopped
4 cups fresh bread crumbs
1 teaspoon salt
2 eggs, beaten
1/2 cup milk
6 bacon slices
1 cup tomato ketchup
1/2 cup chili sauce
1/4 cup Worcestershire sauce

In a bowl, combine celery, onions, raisins, pecans, bread crumbs, salt, and eggs. Stir in milk. Mix well. Lightly salt cavities; stuff cavities with dressing. Place ducks on wire rack in a shallow open pan. Lay 3 bacon slices across breast of each duck. Roast ducks, uncovered, at 500 degrees for 15 minutes. Reduce heat to 325 degrees; continue roasting ducks. About 1/2 hour before end of cooking, remove ducks from oven. Mix ketchup, chili sauce, and Worcestershire sauce in a small bowl; pour sauce over ducks. Return pan to oven; continue roasting until ducks are tender. Total roasting time is about 1 to 1-1/2 hours.

Spur Lake Baked Goose

1 goose, skin on
Salt and pepper
1 recipe Cabinhaus Wild Rice Stuffing (see p. 211)
3 to 4 strips hickory-smoked bacon
3/4 cup water
1 can (10-3/4-ounce) cream of mushroom soup
1 soup can water
1 small garlic clove, minced
1 small onion, chopped fine

Prepare Cabinhaus Wild Rice Stuffing. Lightly sprinkle goose cavity and outside with salt and pepper. Stuff cavity with prepared stuffing. Place any remaining stuffing in buttered casserole; cover and set aside. Place goose, breast side up, in a large baking dish or roaster. Lay bacon strips over breast. Add water to pan. Cover; bake at 325 degrees for 1-1/2 hours.

Combine soup, water, garlic, and onion in a bowl; mix well. Remove pan from oven; drain off accumulated drippings. Discard drippings. Add soup mixture to bottom of pan; return goose to oven. Bake, uncovered, an additional 1-1/2 hours or until tender. Baste occasionally with soup mixture. Bake extra stuffing during last half hour of roasting. To serve goose, discard bacon. Remove goose to a warm serving dish; slice and serve with stuffing. Spoon mushroom sauce over goose slices.

Stir-Fry Wild Duck

4 duck breasts, skin off, boned
2 cups red wine
1 tablespoon cornstarch
1 green or red pepper, seeded
1 large onion, chopped
3 ribs celery
2 tablespoons peanut oil
1 teaspoon salt
1 can (4-ounce) sliced water chestnuts, drained
Dash black pepper

Cut duck breasts into thin strips. Combine red wine and cornstarch in a bowl. Submerge duck strips into wine mixture; marinate for 30 minutes.

Cut vegetables into long, thin strips (julienned). Heat 2 tablespoons oil in a wok or large skillet with high sides. Sear duck strips in wok, turning frequently until cooked. Remove and set aside. Stir-fry green pepper, onion, and celery strips until tender, but still crisp. Add duck and water chestnuts. Heat to serving temperature. Remove duck and vegetables with a slotted spoon to serving dish. Serve over noodles or steamed rice.

Succulent Roast Goose with Dried Fruit Dressing

1 goose 4 to 6 pounds, skin on
Salt and pepper
2 tablespoons brandy
1/2 pound mixed dried fruits
2 cups port wine
1/2 cup dry white wine
2 cups beef broth
2 tablespoons butter or margarine
3/4 cup onion, finely chopped
1/2 teaspoon poultry seasoning
3 to 4 cups fresh bread crumbs
1/3 cup butter or margarine
1/4 cup all-purpose flour
4 slices bacon

The day before cooking, season goose inside and outside with salt and pepper. Sprinkle cavity with brandy. Cover and refrigerate overnight. Place dried fruit in a bowl; pour port wine over fruit. Let stand overnight.

Next day, drain fruit, reserving remaining liquid. In a saucepan, simmer fruit, dry white wine and broth until fruit is tender, about 20 minutes. Strain fruit; reserve liquid. Chop fruit into small pieces; place in a bowl.

Melt 2 tablespoons butter in a skillet; sauté onion until browned. Add onion to chopped fruit mixture; season with poultry seasoning. Return both reserved fruit liquids to skillet; bring to a boil. Reduce heat to medium. Cook, reducing liquid to 1/4 cup. Pour into fruit mixture. Mix in enough bread crumbs to make a soft stuffing. Season with salt and pepper. Stuff goose and close cavity with skewers.

Beat butter and flour together; rub into skin on goose. Cover breast with bacon slices. Place goose on rack in roasting pan, roast for 30 minutes at 475 degrees. Reduce heat to 300 degrees. Continue to roast goose 1-1/2 hours, or until is tender. Baste occasionally with drippings.

To serve, transfer goose to platter. Remove stuffing to separate bowl. Remove surface fat from roaster drippings; strain and measure liquid. Pour into a saucepan. For each cup of liquid, add 1-1/2 tablespoons flour mixed with 2 tablespoons water. Over medium heat, stir in flour mixture; cook until desired consistency. Season with salt and pepper. Serve gravy separately.

Sweet & Sour Goose

1 goose, skin on
1 tablespoon dried sage
1/2 teaspoon salt
1/4 teaspoon pepper
1 large onion, chopped
1 tart apple, cored, quartered
3 to 4 strips maple-flavored bacon
1 cup apple juice
1 can (8-ounce) crushed pineapple, drained
3 tablespoons prepared yellow mustard
1 tablespoon brown sugar

Combine sage, salt, and pepper in a small bowl. Sprinkle goose cavity and out-side with mixture. Stuff goose cavity with onion and apple. Place goose, breast side up, in a large baking dish or medium-sized roaster. Lay bacon strips over breast. Arrange any remaining onion and apple around goose. Add apple juice to pan. Cover; bake at 375 degrees for 2 hours or until tender. Remove stuffing from goose and discard. Discard pan juices.

Process pineapple, mustard, and brown sugar in a blender until smooth. Adjust to suit taste by adding more of one or all sauce ingredients; process. Heat sauce in a saucepan until warm. Serve over sliced goose.

Wild Duck Baked in Wine

2 ducks, breasted, skin off, boned
Flour
Salt and pepper
Olive oil
1 onion, chopped fine
1 cup dry red wine
1/2 cup brandy
1 can (2.25 ounces) sliced ripe olives
2 tablespoons parsley, chopped
1 tablespoon chives, chopped
Salt and pepper

Combine flour, salt and pepper in a plastic zip-top bag. Coat breasts in flour; shake off excess. Heat olive oil in skillet and brown duck breasts on both sides. Lay in a baking dish. Sauté onion in skillet until transparent. Add in remaining ingredients; cook for 1 minute. Adjust seasonings. Pour mixture over breasts. Bake, uncovered, at 350 degrees for about 30 to 45 minutes, or until tender. Baste occasionally with sauce. Serve hot.

Wild Goose with Green Apple Stuffing

1 goose, dressed, skin on
Salt and pepper
1/4 cup lemon juice
1/4 cup butter
1/2 cup onion, finely chopped
1 goose liver, chopped (optional)
1 cup tart green apple, peeled, cored, and diced
1 cup dried apricots, diced
3 cups fresh bread crumbs
6 slices bacon
Melted bacon drippings
1 cup dry red wine

Sprinkle cavity and outside of goose with salt and pepper. Sprinkle lemon juice in cavity.

In a small skillet, melt butter; sauté onion until tender. Add goose liver; cook quickly until browned. Stir in the apple, apricots, and bread crumbs. Salt and pepper, as desired. Stuff goose with mixture. If possible, close cavity and truss. Set goose breast up on a rack in a roasting pan. Cover breast with bacon slices.

Roast in a 325-degree oven approximately 2-1/2 to 3 hours, basting with pan juices. Toward the last hour of roasting, add 1 cup of red wine. Cover during the last hour of cooking.

Wild Goose with Sauerkraut Stuffing

Good served with Red Cabbage and Dumplings

1 goose, dressed, skin on
1 can (29-ounce) sauerkraut with caraway seeds, drained
1 large Granny Smith apple, peeled, cored, chopped fine
1 medium onion, minced
Salt and pepper
1/3 cup bacon drippings
1/2 cup apple juice

In a bowl, mix sauerkraut, apple, and onion. Season goose inside and out with salt and pepper. Stuff cavity with sauerkraut mixture. Close cavity and truss goose. Place breast side up on rack in roasting pan.

Rub bacon drippings all over goose. Add juice to bottom of pan. Cover; roast in a 325-degree oven about 2-1/2 to 3 hours, or until tender. Baste goose occasionally with pan juices. Remove dressing to a bowl before serving.

COOKING

FRESH
FISH

Preparing Your Fish For The Pan

If you are an angler, you know the thrill of the catch and the pleasure of eating a freshly caught fish. However, the flavor and texture of that fish depends largely on how it is handled as soon as it is taken from the water. To ensure great tasting fish, keep your fish alive in the livewell or place them on ice in a cooler until you are ready to clean them. For cleaning fresh fish, the method I prefer is filleting the meat. If a fish is filleted properly, the bones are removed.

Freshwater fish are at their best when cleaned and cooked the day they are taken from the water. But in this era of frozen food, fish may be kept much longer by freezing. When defrosted and prepared, fish can be almost as tasty as the day they were caught. To freeze fish, place the cleaned fillets in an appropriately sized plastic freezer zip-top bag. Fill with enough cold water to cover the fish, press out as much air as possible, seal up the bag, and lay it flat in the freezer. Another method is to place fillets in a milk carton filled with water to cover the fish and then freeze. If the cleaned fish is left whole, double wrap it in freezer wrap. Remember, label and date those packages of fish.

Northern pike and muskie have a slimy film. If you do not fillet these fish, scale them and cut the meat into steaks or leave them whole for baking. To help eliminate the film on the fish steaks, soak them in a saltwater solution. Use 1/2 cup salt to 4 cups cold water; place the fish pieces in this mixture for at least one-half hour. Remove the fish, rinse off the saltwater and wipe off with paper toweling. Prepare with your favorite recipe or package and freeze for use later.

Fish can be prepared in a variety of delicious ways. Most recipes, no matter what fish is specified, will accommodate a substitute you happen to have on hand, especially if the stand-in is of similar flesh color and texture to the one called for in the recipe. Fish is cooked properly when it becomes opaque, but is still moist. If the flesh separates and falls easily into its natural division, the fish is cooked perfectly. Whether broiled, grilled, smoked, baked, or fried, the recipes that follow will help you to enjoy your catch of the day.

1-2-3 Canned Salmon

Use pint canning jars. Wash jars, lids, and rings prior to use. Skin and bone salmon; cut into 2-inch chunks. Pack fish chunks into pint jars.

For each pint jar of salmon, add:

1 tablespoon vinegar
1 tablespoon salt
1 tablespoon cooking oil
1 tablespoon tomato catsup

Mix above ingredients in a container with a pour spout for easy pouring. Increase ingredients times the number of pint jars filled with fish. Seal each jar with a ring. Place jars in a pressure cooker; set pressure at 15 pounds.* When pressure valve begins to jiggle, continue processing for 1 hour and 20 minutes. Remove jars to a draft-free location to cool down. Always make sure jars are sealed before storage.

*Always follow manufacturer's instructions with setting pressure and releasing pressure after processing.

Note: Substitute lake trout. However, omit the 1 tablespoon cooking oil to the ingredients added to jar.

Almondine Walleye

1-1/2 pounds walleye fillets
1/2 cup ground almonds
1/2 cup fresh bread crumbs
1/4 cup canned Italian bread crumbs
1 egg, beaten
2 tablespoons water
1 tablespoon olive oil
1 tablespoon butter

Mix almonds and both kinds of bread crumbs together in a bowl. In a separate bowl, beat egg, add water, and beat again to mix.

Heat olive oil and butter in a skillet. Dip each fillet in egg. Press each side of fillet into almond and bread crumb mixture; brown in skillet. Adjust heat to keep from browning too quickly. Brown both sides. Remove when fish flakes easily with a fork. During browning process, if needed, add more olive oil and butter in equal amounts. Serve hot.

Anytime Baked Fish

4 to 6 fish fillets
2 eggs, beaten
2 tablespoons all-purpose flour
1 teaspoon vegetable oil
1 teaspoon soy sauce
1 cup dry seasoned bread crumbs
3 onions, sliced
1/4 teaspoon celery seed
1 tablespoon butter or margarine
1 tablespoon vegetable oil
Salt and pepper to taste

Combine eggs, flour, 1 teaspoon oil, and soy sauce in a bowl; mix well. Dip fillets in egg mixture. Coat with bread crumbs; place on a plate. Chill for 30 minutes or until time to bake. Place onion slices in a baking pan large enough to fit all fillets. Sprinkle with celery seed; dot with butter. Arrange breaded fish on top of onion slices. Sprinkle with 1 tablespoon vegetable oil, salt and pepper. Bake at 425 degrees for 25 to 30 minutes or until fish flakes easily and breading is crisp and golden brown.

Baked Salmon with Mushroom Stuffing

1 salmon, 3 to 5 pounds
1/2 teaspoon salt
1/8 teaspoon pepper
1 medium onion, chopped
1-1/2 cups fresh mushrooms, sliced
2 tablespoons butter or margarine
1 cup soft bread crumbs
3 tablespoons milk
1 tablespoon parsley flakes
1/4 cup butter or margarine, melted
2 tablespoons fresh lemon juice
1 clove garlic, minced

Rub cavity of salmon with salt and pepper. Sauté onion and mushrooms in 2 tablespoons butter until tender. Add bread crumbs, milk and parsley; stir well. Spoon stuffing mixture into cavity of fish. Close fish lengthwise with skewers. Lace with string to keep stuffing from falling out.

Place salmon in a shallow roasting pan. Mix lemon juice and garlic with butter. Brush top side of fish with this mixture. Bake uncovered in a 325-degree oven, brushing occasionally with butter mixture. Bake until fish flakes easily with a fork, about 1 hour.

Bass Fillets in Beer Sauce

6 bass fillets
2 teaspoons salt
1/4 teaspoon pepper
Paprika
2 tablespoons butter
2 tablespoons flour
2 cups beer
1-1/2 tablespoons brown sugar
4 tablespoons onion, minced
2 cloves (optional)

Sprinkle fillets with salt, pepper and a dash of paprika. Melt butter in a deep skillet. Add flour and stir until lightly browned. Gradually pour in beer, stirring constantly. Bring to boiling point, then lower heat to a simmer. Stir in brown sugar and onions. Arrange fillets in sauce in skillet. Add cloves. Cover loosely and cook about 30 minutes. Fish will flake easily when done. Remove cloves. Place fish on a deep serving dish. Spoon sauce over fillets and serve.

Variation: Substitute walleye or northern.

Bass Fillets with Wild Rice

2 cups cooked wild rice
1 to 2 pounds bass fillets
1 large onion sliced
1 large carrot, peeled and sliced thin
Salt and pepper
Butter

Spray a piece of foil with cooking spray. Layer ingredients in the following order. Spread wild rice on the foil, and then lay the bass fillets on the wild rice. Lay onion slices, then carrot slices on top of fillets. Salt and pepper as desired. Last, add pats of butter over all. Package up the foil making an air-tight packet. Lay packet on a baking sheet. Bake at 325 degrees for 30 to 40 minutes, or until fish flakes easily.

Note: The amounts of wild rice and fillets can vary, however, the order in layering should stay the same. The foil pack can also be baked on the grill.

Blackened Mississippi Catfish

2 large catfish fillets (2 to 3 pounds total)
4 tablespoons paprika
2 tablespoons dried oregano
1 tablespoon dried basil
1 teaspoon salt
1 teaspoon freshly ground black pepper
1/2 teaspoon ground red pepper
3 tablespoons olive oil

Combine dry ingredients in a bowl. Sprinkle mixture over both sides of fillets. Heat oil in a large cast iron skillet over high heat. Add fillets; cook 4 to 5 minutes on each side or until fish flakes easily with a fork.

Breaded Salmon Loaf

A delicious option for using leftover salmon

3 cups salmon, cooked and flaked
14 soda crackers, crushed
2 eggs, slightly beaten
1 tablespoon fresh parsley, minced
1 teaspoon onion, minced
2 tablespoons lemon juice
1 teaspoon Dijon mustard
1 cup milk
Salt and pepper, to taste
3/4 cup soft bread crumbs
2 tablespoons butter, melted

In a medium-sized bowl, mix salmon, parsley, onion, lemon juice, mustard, eggs, salt and pepper. In a small bowl, mix crushed crackers with milk. Pour into salmon mixture. Mix well to distribute milk and crackers throughout. Spray a loaf or bread pan with vegetable spray. Press salmon mixture into pan. Sprinkle bread crumbs over the top to just lightly cover. Drizzle melted butter on top of crumbs. Bake for 40 to 50 minutes. Serve slices of salmon loaf with Old Fashioned Cheese Sauce (see p. 249).

Broiled Coho Salmon

1 salmon, 3 to 5 pounds
4 tablespoons butter
1/2 teaspoon seasoned salt
1/4 teaspoon garlic powder
1 tablespoon parsley or parsley flakes
1/4 teaspoon Worcestershire sauce
Dash of fresh ground black pepper

Cut salmon in half, butterfly fashion, splitting back rib bone. Cut off bottom belly fat and discard. On a greased baking sheet, lay salmon skin side down. Melt butter in a small saucepan; stir in next 5 ingredients. Liberally brush salmon with melted butter mixture.

Arrange oven rack approximately 5 inches from broiler coils; broil salmon about 8 to 10 minutes. Salmon should take on a brown, slightly crusty appearance as it broils. Salmon is done when it flakes easily at its thickest point.

Note: Cut salmon into 1 inch steaks. Follow recipe.

Broiled Sesame Trout

6 serving-size rainbow trout, dressed
1/2 cup lemon juice
4 teaspoons salt
1/4 teaspoon pepper
1/3 cup sesame seed
3/4 cup butter or margarine

With a sharp knife make 3 light slashes on each side of fish, without cutting flesh too deep. Mix lemon juice, salt, and pepper in a 9-by 13-inch baking pan. Add fish and turn over, coating both sides with marinade. Cover with plastic wrap and refrigerate for 3 hours. Turn fish occasionally. Toast sesame seeds in a small saucepan until golden. Stir occasionally. Add butter and heat until melted.

Place fish on broiler pan rack. Drain marinade from baking pan into sesame seed mixture; blend. Broil fish 3 to 4 inches from heat, about 5 minutes on each side. Baste frequently with sesame seed mixture. Fish is done when easily flaked with a fork. Remove fish with a pancake turner to warm platter, spoon hot juices over trout.

Brown Trout with Cranberry Pecan Butter Sauce

2 tablespoons cooking oil
2 pounds brown trout fillets
1/2 teaspoon salt
1/4 teaspoon black pepper
5 tablespoons butter
1/2 teaspoon dried sage
1/2 cup pecans, finely chopped
1/4 cup green onions, chopped
1/4 cup dried cranberries (craisins)
2 tablespoons fresh parsley, chopped

In a large nonstick frying pan, heat 1 tablespoon oil over moderate heat. Sprinkle fish with salt and pepper. Place half of the trout in pan and fry for 2 minutes. Gently turn trout; continue to cook until browned and just about done. Remove fish to cookie sheet and keep warm in 250-degree oven. Add remaining 1 tablespoon oil to frying pan. Cook remainder of fillets in the same manner as before. Place on cookie sheet and return to oven.

Wipe out frying pan with paper toweling. Melt butter over low heat. Add sage, pecans, green onions and dried cranberries. Stir mixture until butter has turned a golden brown, approximately 5 minutes. Stir in fresh parsley. To serve, spoon butter sauce over each trout fillet.

Variation: Substitute walleye or lake trout.

Buttermilk Deep-Fried Walleye

3 pounds walleye fillets
Buttermilk
1 lemon, sliced
2 cups vegetable oil
2 cups Bisquick mix
2-1/2 cups club soda or beer

Place fillets in a bowl or casserole dish. Add buttermilk to cover fillets. Lay several lemon slices on top of fillets. Cover and refrigerate for two to three hours.

Drain fillets and cut in half if too large. Heat 2 cups vegetable oil to 375 degrees, in a deep fryer, heavy cast-iron skillet, or 2-1/2-quart heavy saucepan. In a bowl, combine Bisquick mix with club soda or beer, until the consistency is like buttermilk. Dip fillets into batter. Let excess batter drip off into bowl. Deep fry fillets until golden brown. Remove; drain on paper toweling. Transfer fillets to a pan and place in 200-degree oven to keep warm. Continue frying remainder of fillets.

Variation: 1) Substitute self-rising flour in place of Bisquick.
Variation: 2) Substitute northern or perch.

Cabinhaus Poached Northern Pike

1 northern pike, cut steaks or fillets
1 to 2 quarts water
1 tablespoon salt
1 large onion, sliced
1 to 2 carrots, peeled and sliced
1 to 2 stalks celery cut into 1-inch chunks
Handful of celery tops
3 sprigs of fresh parsley
2 bay leaves
1/2 teaspoon thyme
1/2 teaspoon basil
8 to 10 whole peppercorns
1-1/2 cups white wine or 1/2 cup white vinegar
Butter, melted

Fit a Dutch oven or large pot with a rack. A round cake cooling rack will work. Place vegetables on rack. Add herbs, salt and enough water to generously cover vegetables. *Do not add the wine.* Over medium heat, bring ingredients to a slow simmer. Simmer until carrots are just tender, about 12 to 15 minutes. Stir in wine or vinegar. Lay northern steaks on rack. Bring back to a slow simmer and continue poaching. The fish is cooked when it appears white.

Remove fish from liquid with a slotted spoon. Place on a heated serving dish. Garnish with poached vegetables. Serve fish with melted butter for dipping.

Rule of thumb for cooking fish: Cook 10 minutes for each inch of thickness for fresh fish; 20 minutes for frozen.

Catfish Cakes

2 pounds catfish fillets
Water
1/2 cup pancake mix
4 tablespoons mayonnaise
2 tablespoons onion, minced
1 egg, beaten
1/4 teaspoon seasoned salt
1/8 teaspoon pepper
1/2 teaspoon Worcestershire sauce
2 cups fresh bread crumbs
4 to 6 tablespoons butter or margarine

Place fillets in a large skillet or Dutch oven. Add water, barely covering fillets. Poach until fillets turn white. Remove from skillet with a slotted spoon to a colander; drain off excess water. Discard water. Cool down; remove any remaining bones. Flake meat in a bowl. Add in pancake mix, mayonnaise, onion, egg, seasoned salt, pepper, and Worcestershire sauce. Make a small test cake. If cake will not hold shape, add more pancake mix, a little at a time. Place bread crumbs in a shallow bowl or plate. Form mixture into 3-inch cakes; dipping both sides of each cake into bread crumbs. Set aside.

Melt butter in skillet over moderate heat. Fry cakes until heated through and golden brown on both sides, turning once with a spatula to brown second side.

Leftover fish?
Cut into bite-sized pieces
and use as a topping
for a salad

Cheesy Fish Casserole

1-1/2 cups milk
2 tablespoons butter or margarine
1 cup fresh bread crumbs
1/4 cup onion, minced
1-1/2 cups shredded Cheddar cheese
2 tablespoons fresh parsley, snipped
Salt and pepper
Dash paprika
3 eggs, well beaten
2 cups flaked, cooked fish (salmon, whitefish, walleye, northern, muskie)

Heat milk and butter in a saucepan until butter melts. Pour over bread crumbs in mixing bowl. Add onion, cheese, parsley, salt, pepper, and paprika. Mix well. Stir in beaten eggs. Spray a 1-1/2 quart casserole with nonstick cooking spray. Arrange flaked fish in casserole; pour cheese mixture over fish. Set casserole in a larger pan filled with warm water to within 1 inch of the top of casserole. Bake at 325 degrees 1-1/4 hours, or until a table knife inserted in the center is clean when removed. Serve with Easy Mushroom Sauce. (See p. 244)

Cheesy Mushroom-Stuffed Trout

1/3 cup green onion, chopped
1 cup fresh mushrooms, sliced, grated
2 tablespoons Parmesan cheese
Salt and pepper
1/2 fresh lemon, sliced thin
2 pounds whole trout (brook, brown, or rainbow)

Combine onion, mushrooms, and cheese. Spoon mixture into cavity of each fish. Season with salt and pepper. Lay lemon slices on top of mixture. Close cavities with toothpicks to keep stuffing inside. Broil about 5 to 10 minutes per side, until fish flakes. Remove lemon slices from cavity before serving. Garnish fish with fresh cut lemon slices or wedges.

Chill Chaser Chowder

Delicious after a wintery day spent enjoying the outdoors

1 pound fish, cleaned (sunfish, crappies, bass, or northern)
2 cups water
1 bay leaf
5 whole allspice
1/8 teaspoon thyme
Several sprigs of fresh parsley, minced
3 small carrots, chopped
1 medium onion, chopped
2 medium peeled potatoes, diced
1/2 cup frozen peas
1/2 cup frozen corn
1 pint half-and-half
Salt and pepper to taste
Dash or two of hot pepper sauce (optional)

Add first 6 ingredients to a soup pot. Bring to a boil; reduce heat and keep ingredients at a gentle boil until fish flakes easily. Remove fish with a slotted spoon to colander and drain. Remove any bones and skin. Strain fish liquid and save. Discard spices, bones, and skin from fish.

Return fish meat and strained broth to the kettle. Add the vegetables and half-and-half to kettle; stir to blend. Simmer until vegetables are tender. Salt and pepper to taste.

Cornmeal-Crusted Trout

Crispy and flavorful

4 (12-ounce) butterflied trout
6 bacon slices, chopped
2 cups yellow cornmeal
2 teaspoons seasoned salt
1 teaspoon garlic powder
1/4 teaspoon pepper

Fry bacon until crisp, in a large skillet over medium-high heat. Remove bacon; set aside. Stir together cornmeal and next 4 ingredients; dredge trout in mixture. Cook trout in skillet in bacon drippings, 4 to 6 minutes on each side, or until fish flakes with a fork. Crumble bacon; sprinkle over trout before serving.

Crab Stuffed Walleye

Company-pleasing fare

2 pounds large walleye fillets
1/4 cup onion, chopped
1/4 cup butter
1 can (4-ounce) mushrooms, drained (reserve liquid)
1 can (7-1/2-ounce) crab meat, drained and chopped
1/2 cup saltine crackers crumbs
2 tablespoons fresh parsley, snipped
1/2 teaspoon salt
Dash of pepper

Sauce:
3 tablespoons butter or margarine
3 tablespoons flour
1/4 teaspoon salt
Reserved mushroom liquid and milk (1-1/2 cups)
1/3 cup dry white wine
4 ounces Swiss cheese, shredded
1/2 teaspoon paprika

In a skillet, sauté onion in butter until tender, but not brown. Stir mushrooms, crab, cracker crumbs, parsley, salt and pepper into skillet.

Spray a baking pan or casserole dish with vegetable oil. Lay one fillet on bottom of pan. Spread mixture over fillet, reserving enough for remaining fillets. Lay second fillet on top of mixture. Repeat process with until all fillets are used.

To make sauce, melt butter in a saucepan; blend in flour and salt. Add milk to reserved mushroom liquid to make 1-1/2 cups. Cook over low temperature. Blend wine into saucepan. Stir until mixture thickens and bubbles. Pour sauce over stuffed fillets in baking pan.

Bake at 400 degrees for 25 minutes. Remove, sprinkle Swiss cheese and paprika over fillets. Return to oven; bake an additional 10 minutes or until fish flakes easily with fork.

Sally Willman, Three Lakes, WI

Crappie Fillet Loaf

Good way to top off a day of crappie fishing

Crappie fillets
6 to 8 tablespoons butter or margarine
1 cup fine bread crumbs
1 large onion, chopped fine
1/2 cup celery, minced
1 green pepper, chopped fine
Salt and pepper
1-1/2 cups sour cream
2 tablespoons dry dill weed

Butter sides and bottom of loaf pan. Line bottom of pan with bread crumbs. Lay alternate layers of fillets, onion, celery, and green pepper in pan. Season each layer with a small amount of salt and pepper; spread on a light layer of sour cream. Sprinkle with dry dill weed. Continue layering. For the last layer, place a heavy coating of sour cream on top.

Bake uncovered for 30 minutes at 350 degrees or until top layer is golden. Work knife around pan to loosen loaf. Remove loaf gently from pan so it doesn't break apart. Sprinkle with more dill weed if desired. Cut loaf into thick slices and serve with tartar sauce and lemon wedges.

Creamy Baked Walleye

1-1/2 to 2 pounds walleye fillets
1 to 2 sticks butter or margarine
1/2 pint whipping cream
Salt and pepper

Place one stick of butter in a 9- by 13-inch cake pan; melt butter in the oven. Add more butter until melted butter completely covers bottom of pan. Lay fillets in melted butter. Pour whipping cream over fillets; salt and pepper to taste.

Bake in a 325-degree oven for 30 minutes or until fillets are flaky. Remove from oven; place fillets in a serving dish with sides; spoon pan juices over fish. Garnish with parsley sprigs and serve.

Variation: Substitute northern pike or bass.

Creole Fish

1 pound fish fillets, cut up (crappies, perch, northern or bass)
1/2 cup water
1/2 cup onion, chopped
1/2 cup green pepper, chopped
1 clove garlic, minced
1 can (16-ounce) diced tomatoes, undrained
1 tablespoon chicken bouillon
2 tablespoons fresh parsley, chopped
Dash or two hot pepper sauce
1/2 cup hot water
1 tablespoon cornstarch
3 tablespoons cold water

In a large saucepan, combine 1/2 cup water, garlic, onion, and green pepper. Cover, and simmer until vegetables are tender. Add parsley, bouillon, pepper sauce, tomatoes, and 1/2 cup hot water. Continue to simmer mixture for an additional 10 minutes.

Blend cornstarch and cold water in a small bowl. Stir slowly into sauce. Keep heat at a simmer. Stir until sauce has thickened. Add fish and cook for 5 minutes longer, or until fish is cooked. Season to taste; add more pepper sauce if needed.

If Creole mixture becomes too thick, thin it with tomato juice or tomato sauce until it reaches desired consistency. Serve over hot white rice.

Crispy Grilled Walleye Fillets

3/4 cup cornflakes, finely crushed
1/3 cup sesame seed, toasted
4 to 6 walleye fillets
4 tablespoons soy sauce
Salt
Pepper
1/2 cup sour cream with chives

Combine cornflakes and sesame seeds in a bowl. Brush walleye fillets with soy sauce. Season with salt and pepper. Spread one side of each fillet with sour cream. Press coated side in cornflake mixture. Repeat process with other side of fillets. Place fillet in a well-greased wire grill basket. Grill fish over medium-hot heat about 8 minutes. Turn basket to other side; grill fillets until they flake easily, about 5 to 8 minutes longer.

Crispy Salmon Steaks

1/2 cup butter
1 teaspoon salt
1/8 teaspoon paprika
6 salmon steaks (6 to 8 ounces) 3/4 inch thick
1 cup crushed Ritz crackers
1 cup crushed potato chips
6 lemon wedges
6 parsley sprigs

Melt butter; add salt and paprika. Set aside. Mix cracker and potato chip crumbs together in a bowl. Set aside. Wipe steaks with damp paper toweling. Dip each steak into butter mixture; then roll in cracker and chip crumbs.

Lightly spray broiler pan with vegetable cooking oil; arrange steaks on pan. Broil 6 inches from heat for 5 minutes. Turn steaks over and broil second side for 5 to 8 minutes longer or until fish flakes easily with a fork.

Deep-Fried Crispy Smelt

2 pounds cleaned smelt (about 15 per pound)
1-1/2 cups flour
1/2 cup fresh Parmesan cheese, grated
1 can (5-ounce) tomato sauce
Dash or two of hot pepper sauce
Vegetable oil
Salt and pepper
Cocktail sauce
Lemon wedges

Wash and dry smelt. Combine flour, salt, pepper, and cheese. Add dash or two of hot pepper sauce to tomato sauce. Dip smelt in tomato sauce, and then roll in flour mixture. Heat oil to 350 degrees. Place smelt in a single layer in fry basket or electric skillet. Fry for 3 to 4 minutes or until golden brown. Drain fish on paper toweling. Salt and pepper, if desired. Place cooked smelt in a warm oven and continue frying remainder. Serve with cocktail sauce and lemon wedges.

Devilish Perch

1/4 cup steak sauce
1/2 cup Worcestershire sauce
1/2 cup water
1/4 cup lemon juice
2 tablespoons dry mustard
1 teaspoon chili powder
1 teaspoon pepper
1/4 teaspoon cayenne pepper
2 pounds perch fillets
Buttered bread crumbs

Marinate the fillets 45 minutes to one hour in a mixture of the first eight ingredients. Remove fish; discard marinade. Arrange fillets in a greased baking dish. Cover and bake at 350 degrees for 15 minutes or until fish flakes easily.

When fish is done, crumble buttered bread crumbs over fillets. Place under the broiler and brown bread crumbs. Serve fillets with mustard or tartar sauce.

*To grill, use a wire grill basket.
It works great to keep fish
intact when turned.*

Disappearing Fish Patties

They disappear faster than you can cook them

4 to 5 pounds walleye, northern, or bass fillets, diced
2 eggs
1 cup pancake flour or Bisquick mix
1/2 medium onion, chopped fine
1/4 medium green pepper, chopped fine (optional)
3/4 cup milk
Paprika, dash
Garlic salt, dash
Salt and pepper to taste
1 tablespoon vegetable oil
1 teaspoon butter or margarine

Dice fish in 1/4 to 1/2 inch square pieces. In a bowl, beat eggs until frothy; mix in flour, onion, green pepper, and diced fish. Add milk a little at a time until the mixture is the consistency of potato salad. More pancake flour or milk can be added if mixture is too runny or too thick. Add seasonings.

Preheat griddle or frying pan to 325 degrees; lightly coat with vegetable oil and butter. Fry a small amount of mixture; taste and adjust seasonings if necessary. Shape mixture into round patties about 1/2 inch thick; dust lightly with pancake flour. Fry until golden brown on both sides. Serve with tartar sauce or lemon wedges.

Edie's Tasty Fish Chowder

1 cup potatoes, peeled and diced
1 can (14-1/2-ounce) chicken broth
2 strips bacon, diced
1 medium onion, diced
3 ribs celery, diced
Butter or margarine
Flour, all-purpose
2 cups milk or half-and-half
1/3 cup frozen corn
1/2 cup canned diced tomatoes, drained
1 pound fish fillets, cut into bite-size chunks
1/4 teaspoon thyme
1 tablespoon parsley, fresh chopped, or dried
Salt and pepper to taste
Dash of Tabasco sauce (optional)

Cover potatoes with broth; simmer until tender. Remove potatoes with a slotted spoon to a bowl; set aside. Save broth. In a large kettle, cook bacon until slightly crisp. Add butter, onion, and celery; sauté until onions are transparent.

Add flour, stirring constantly until slightly browned, approximately 5 to 6 minutes. Gradually add saved broth. Continue stirring until thickened and smooth. Add milk and simmer on low heat about 10 minutes.

Blend in corn, potatoes and drained tomatoes. Add fish chunks and seasonings. Simmer until fish turns white, which will take about 5 to 7 minutes, depending on size of chunks. Season chowder with salt and pepper.

Fillets Thermidor

3 pounds fish fillets (walleye, northern)
2-1/4 cups whole milk
1-1/2 teaspoons salt
1/8 teaspoon pepper
1/2 cup butter
1/2 cup all-purpose flour
1/2 pound process sharp Cheddar cheese, coarsely grated
1/2 cup sherry
Paprika

Roll up each fillet; insert a toothpick to keep from unrolling. Stand on end in a baking pan. Pour milk over fish; sprinkle with salt and pepper. Bake uncovered at 350 degrees, about 30 or 40 minutes, or until easily flaked with fork. Remove from oven.

Preheat broiler. Remove liquid from pan and save. Melt butter in a small saucepan; stir in flour. Slowly stir in saved liquid. Cook, stirring until thickened. Add cheese, stirring until melted. Add lemon juice to sauce; pour over fillets. Sprinkle top with paprika. Quickly brown fillets under broiler.

Fish Cakes

Great sandwich fare hot or cold

1 egg
1-1/2 pounds cold cooked fish, shredded
1 cup mashed potatoes
1/4 cup onion, minced
1/4 cup celery, minced
1/4 teaspoon seasoned salt
Dash of garlic salt
Pepper
1/2 cup Bisquick or pancake flour
1 to 2 tablespoons vegetable oil
1/2 tablespoon butter or margarine

Beat egg; stir in next seven ingredients. Mixture will be soft. Gradually add in the Bisquick until mixture is firm enough to handle. It should hold its shape when made into a patty cake. If the mixture becomes too firm, add a little milk until it reaches the right consistency. Pan-fry cakes in heated oil and butter, until a deep golden brown on both sides.

Serve fish cakes with tartar sauce or a white sauce spooned over top. To serve as a hot sandwich, use a hamburger bun spread with mayonnaise or tartar sauce; top cake with a slice of tomato and lettuce.

Spray wire grill basket with a nonstick spray before using. This keeps fish from sticking to the basket and cleanup easier.

Fish & Chips

The chips are the breading

1 pound walleye, perch or northern fillets
1/4 cup milk
1 cup potato chips, crushed
1/4 cup grated Parmesan cheese
1/4 teaspoon dried thyme
1 tablespoon dry bread crumbs or cracker crumbs
2 tablespoons butter or margarine, melted

Cut fish into serving size pieces. Place milk in a shallow bowl. In another shallow bowl, combine potato chips, Parmesan cheese and thyme. Dip fish in milk, then coat with potato chip mixture. Sprinkle a greased 8-inch square baking dish with bread or cracker crumbs. Place fish over crumbs; drizzle fish with butter. Bake, uncovered at 400 degrees for 12 to 14 minutes or until fish flakes easily with a fork.

Sally Willman, Three Lakes, WI

Fish Salad Sandwich Spread

A great way to use leftover fried, baked, or poached fillets

2 cups cooked fish, flaked
1 cup mayonnaise
1/2 cup celery, finely chopped
2 tablespoons onion, minced
2 tablespoons dill pickle, finely chopped
2 hard-cooked eggs, finely diced
Dash pepper
Tomato slices
Shredded lettuce

Combine all ingredients in a bowl, with the exception of the lettuce and tomatoe slices. Be careful not to break the fish into chunks that are too small. Mix thoroughly to blend the flavors. Refrigerate.

To use, spread on your favorite type of bread or roll and top with a tomato slice and shredded lettuce.

Fish Timbales

2 eggs, well beaten
2 cups leftover fish, chunked
1/2 cup celery, minced
1 teaspoon paprika
1 teaspoon Worcestershire sauce
1 tablespoon lemon juice
1-1/2 cups milk
1 cup uncooked quick-rolled oats
Salt and pepper

Thoroughly combine all ingredients in a bowl. Salt and pepper mixture. Evenly divide mixture into 6 greased custard cups or use a 9- by 5-inch loaf pan. Bake at 350 degrees for 50 to 60 minutes or until firm to touch. Unmold and serve with Easy Mushroom Sauce (see p. 244) or Egg Sauce (see p. 245).

Friday Night Fish Fry

Fish fillets (walleye, perch, northern, or crappie)
1/4 cup all-purpose flour
1/4 cup cornstarch
Salt and pepper
1/4 cup beer
2 egg whites

Sift flour, cornstarch, salt and pepper into a bowl. Stir in beer. Separate egg whites from yolks. Discard yolks or save for another recipe. Beat egg whites until stiff. Just before frying fillets, fold egg whites into batter mixture with a spatula.

Heat oil in a heavy skillet or deep fryer. Dip fillets into batter; drain off excess. Fry in hot oil until golden brown on each side. Remove with a spatula. Lay on paper toweling in a baking pan, and keep warm in a 150-degree oven until ready to serve. Continue frying until all fillets are browned. Serve fillets along with Tangy Slaw (See p. 238) and Green Onion Tartar Sauce (see p. 246).

Garden Vegetable Topped Walleye

1 small clove garlic, minced
1/2 cup minced green onion
1/2 cup green pepper, chopped
1/2 cup celery, chopped
4 large Roma tomatoes, coarsely chopped
3 tablespoons fresh parsley, snipped
3 tablespoons butter
Salt and pepper
2 to 3 pounds walleye fillets

Mix first 6 ingredients in a bowl. Melt butter; spread in bottom of shallow baking dish. Lay fillets on bottom of pan. Lightly salt and pepper. Spread vegetable mixture over top of fillets. Bake in a 325-degree oven until fish flakes easily with a fork.

Variation: Substitute northern, perch, crappie.

Garlic Trout with Dried Tomatoes

2 pounds lake trout fillets
3/4 cup olive oil
4 cloves garlic, minced fine
1 lemon, sliced thin
1 medium onion, sliced thin
1/2 cup dried tomatoes in olive oil, drained, cut in pieces
1/2 teaspoon fresh rosemary, cut fine

Cut fillets into 2-inch sized pieces. Heat olive oil in a large skillet over medium heat. Add garlic, lemon, onion, dried tomatoes, and rosemary. Cook covered, for 5 minutes. Add trout. Cook, covered, for 5 minutes. Turn pieces over. Depending on thickness of fillets, cover and cook for 10 to 20 minutes longer or until fish flakes easily.

Golden Fried Perch

1 pound perch fillets
1/8 cup milk
1 cup packaged breading mix
1/4 cup cornmeal
1/8 teaspoon garlic powder
1/4 teaspoon hot'n spicy Creole seasoning
1/8 teaspoon dried parsley flakes (optional)
1 egg
2 to 3 tablespoons olive oil

Wash and dry fish. Beat milk and egg until foamy. Mix together the breading mix, cornmeal, garlic salt, and Creole seasoning in a shallow container. Dip fillets in egg mixture, then coat with breading mix. In a large fry pan or electric skillet, heat oil. Fry fish until crisp and golden on both sides. Cook until fish flakes easily with a fork. Remove, drain on paper toweling. Transfer to a heated platter. Garnish with lemon wedges and serve with tartar sauce.

Grandma's Quick Fish Chowder

Use up those frozen fish fillets

6 cups milk
1 package (10-ounce) frozen corn
1 package (9-ounce) frozen peas
2 pounds fresh or frozen fish fillets, cut into 2-inch pieces
1 tablespoon dried thyme
1-1/2 teaspoons onion powder
1 teaspoon dried basil
1-1/2 cups instant mashed potato flakes
Salt and pepper

In a large pot, combine all ingredients, except potato flakes. Bring to a boil over medium heat. Reduce heat to low; simmer for 15 to 20 minutes. Stir in potato flakes; simmer for 5 minutes, or until thickened. If soup gets too thick, add more milk to thin. Serve immediately.

Grilled Marinated Trout

1 large trout, cavity cleaned
Large wedge of lemon
Combination of parsley, basil, rosemary, or chives in any amount
  (your preference)

Marinade:

1/2 cup soy sauce
1/2 cup white sherry
1 tablespoon lime or lemon juice
1/4 cup olive oil
2 cloves garlic, minced
1/2 teaspoon seasoned salt
1/8 teaspoon black pepper

Combine all marinade ingredients in a bowl or a shaker-type container and mix or shake well.

Brush trout cavity with juice from lemon wedge; sprinkle cavity with the combination of herbs. Lay trout in a shallow pan; pour marinade over the trout. Let stand for one hour, turning once. Remove trout from marinade. Strain marinade and set aside. Spray a wire grill basket with nonstick cooking spray. Lay trout in basket.

Grill should be at medium-hot heat. Cook over hot coals. Baste trout with marinade during grilling. Turn over and grill evenly on both sides. Trout is done when it flakes easily with a fork.

Grilled Muskie with Wild Rice Stuffing

1 muskie, cleaned and scaled

Remove head and also tail and fins if you wish. Remove membrane bloodline; wash cavity and outside thoroughly. Dry with paper toweling to remove any slime. Salt and pepper inside cavity. (Continues on p. 182)

Wild Rice Stuffing

3 to 4 cups cooked wild rice
1/4 stick butter
1 cup celery, chopped
1 medium onion, chopped
1 can (8-ounce) sliced mushrooms, drained
2 chicken bouillon cubes
1/4 cup hot water
Pepper
1/2 teaspoon poultry seasoning
1 can (10-3/4-ounce) cream of mushroom soup
1 medium onion, sliced
1 lemon sliced thin
Butter

Melt butter in a large skillet. Sauté celery and onions until tender. Add mushrooms and heat. Dissolve bouillon cubes in hot water; mix with mushroom soup. Stir into skillet. Add in wild rice and seasonings as needed. Do not stuff fish until you are ready to bake it. Bake any stuffing not used in fish separately in a casserole dish. Serve as a side dish.

Grilling: On a flat surface, wrap muskie in heavy-duty aluminum foil. If foil is not wide enough, place two foil sheets together. To create a seam, fold edges together on the one side several times. Open foil. This will be your bottom piece. Lay another piece of foil on top of this. Place fish in middle of foil. Loosely stuff fish with wild rice mixture. If possible, use metal skewers to close cavity and lace with string. Place onion slices on top of fish, then cover with thin lemon slices. Top with pats of butter. Close foil tightly around fish, sealing so juices will not escape.

Have charcoal grill at 350 to 400 degrees. Bank coals on sides distributing heat evenly. Place fish on grill, cover and bake. Do not let temperature drop below 325 degrees. Grill until fish flakes easily from the thickest part of fish. Transfer to a large serving platter. Before serving, remove cooked onions and lemon. Remove skin from top of fish and any visible bones. Slice thick lemon pieces and place around fish; garnish with small pieces of parsley dipped in paprika.

Note: For a 10-pound muskie (cleaned weight) bake for 2-1/2 to 3 hours. Rule of thumb is 15 to 20 minutes per pound.

Variation: Substitute northern.

Grilled Salmon and Vegetables

1 cup green onions, minced
1 can (8 ounces) mushrooms, drained
3 medium carrots, diced
2 cups cleaned potatoes, skin on, diced
1 teaspoon fresh parsley
1 cup chicken broth
Salmon fillet or 6 salmon steaks (about 2 pounds total)

In a saucepan, cook onions, mushrooms, carrots, parsley, and potatoes in the broth until vegetables are almost tender. Do not drain off liquid.

Cover the bottom of a baking pan with heavy foil. (Saves bottom of pan from blackening during grilling.) Spray pan with a butter-flavored cooking spray. Lay fish in center of pan. Salt and pepper salmon. Arrange vegetable mixture and liquid around fish.

Preheat charcoal or gas grill to a medium heat. Place baking pan with fish and vegetables on top grill rack. Close cover on grill. Grill about 20 to 30 minutes, or until fish flakes with a fork.

Italian Baked Bass

2 to 3 pounds bass, filleted
2 green peppers, seeded and chopped
1 can (8-ounce) sliced mushrooms, drained
1 onion, minced
1 cup celery, chopped
1 bay leaf, crushed
1/4 cup butter
2-1/2 cups canned, Italian stewed tomatoes, undrained
1/2 teaspoon dried basil
1/2 teaspoon dried rosemary
1/2 teaspoon dried oregano
Salt, as needed
3 to 4 bacon slices

Use a medium skillet to melt butter. Simmer peppers, mushrooms, onion, and celery in butter until tender. Add tomatoes, bay leaf, and dried herbs to vegetable mixture; salt as needed. Heat mixture to boiling. Remove from heat.

Arrange fish fillets in a 9- by 13-inch baking pan. Pour tomato mixture over fish. Cover, bake at 400 degrees for 15 minutes. Uncover; place bacon slices over fish. Return to oven. Continue to bake uncovered, at 400 degrees for 25 to 30 minutes longer. Baste occasionally. Fish will be done when easily flaked with a fork but still moist.

Italian Marinated Salmon Fillets

1 to 2 pounds salmon fillets skinned
1 tablespoon fresh lemon juice
1/4 cup olive oil
1 teaspoon salt
1/8 teaspoon black pepper
1/8 teaspoon ground turmeric
1 medium-sized clove garlic, chopped
2 to 3 tablespoons Italian salad dressing
4 thin lemon slices

Cut salmon fillets into 4 inch pieces. Place fillets in a non-metallic container or plastic zip-top bag. Mix lemon juice, olive oil, salt, pepper, turmeric, garlic and Italian salad dressing in a bowl. Pour over fillets. It is okay if marinade does not completely cover fillets. Place lemon slices on top of fillets. If using a bowl, cover with plastic wrap. Refrigerate and marinate fillets 24 hours, turning several times.

Preheat gas grill at lowest setting. Remove fillets from marinade and drain. Discard marinade. Lay fillets in a wire grill basket; grill over low heat. Grill about 10 to 20 minutes until fish flakes easily.

Dr. Eric Swanson, Cable, WI

Jo's Stella Lake Chowder

2 pounds potatoes, peeled and cubed
1/4 cup butter
3/4 cup onion, minced
2 cans (10-3/4-ounce) cream of potato soup
1-1/2 cups real cream
1/2 cup whole milk
1/2 pound fish cut in small chunks
2 cans (2.25-ounce) clams, drained
Salt and pepper to taste

Cook potatoes in boiling water until tender; drain, and set aside. Melt butter in soup kettle and sauté onions until transparent. Add in potatoes, cream of potato soup, cream, milk, and fish pieces. Cover and simmer about 15 minutes. Add clams and heat thoroughly. Serve.

Note: If you wish to use less cream, replace the amount with milk.

Krispie Baked Fillets

1 to 1-1/2 pounds fish fillets (walleye, perch, northern)
3 tablespoons mayonnaise
3/4 teaspoon dried Italian seasoning
1/4 teaspoon salt
1/4 teaspoon pepper
3/4 cup Rice Krispies cereal, crumbed

In a small bowl, stir together mayonnaise, dried seasoning, salt, and pepper. Spread over fillets. Coat fillets on both sides in cereal crumbs. Lay fillets in a single layer, on a lightly greased baking sheet. Bake at 450 degrees for 10 minutes or until fish flakes with a fork. Serve with lemon wedges.

Mom's Pickled Fish

An all-time favorite recipe

Northern fillets, fresh or frozen northern
Canning salt
White vinegar

If using frozen fillets, defrost. Cut fish into small pieces. To measure how much fish you have, pack fish in a quart jar. Then empty contents into a large enough bowl. For each quart jar of fish measured, add 5/8 cup canning salt to bowl. Cover salted fish with white vinegar. Refrigerate for five days. Each day stir fish once. After five days, remove fish and drain; wash well to remove all salt. Let fish stand in cold water for one hour. Drain well.

Pickling mixture:

For each quart of fish, in a kettle, mix:

1 cup white vinegar
1 cup white sugar
1 cup white sherry wine
1/4 cup pickling spices

Bring mixture to a boil; remove and cool mixture.

Pack fish pieces in clean jars in layers, as follows – fish, sliced onions. Repeat layers until jar is filled to 1/4 inch from top. Fill with pickling mixture. Seal jars. Refrigerate for at least 24 hours before eating.

Oven Crisp Tater Fish

1/4 cup butter or margarine
1 to 1-1/4 cups packaged mashed potato flakes
2 pounds northern or walleye fillets
1 egg, slightly beaten
1/4 cup milk
Paprika
Garlic salt
Salt and pepper

Melt margarine in shallow baking pan in which fish will fit easily without crowding. Place potato flakes in a bowl, add a scant 1/4 teaspoon of paprika, a dash of garlic salt, and salt and pepper. Mix coating. Beat egg and add in milk, beating until frothy.

Cut fish into pieces, or "fingers," about 3 inches long and 1 inch wide. Dip fish first in egg mixture, then coat with potato flakes. Arrange pieces in prepared pan. Make sure not to crowd the fish. Bake at 475 degrees for 5 minutes. Turn fish over with a spatula being careful not to break pieces. Return to oven for 2 to 5 minutes until coating turns a deep golden brown and fish flakes easily in the thickest part.

Oven-Fried Fillets

1-1/2 to 2 pounds walleye, perch, northern, or smallmouth bass fillets
4 tablespoons butter or margarine, melted
1/2 teaspoon paprika
3/4 cup Ritz crackers, crushed
3 tablespoons grated Parmesan cheese
1 tablespoon dried parsley
1/2 teaspoon Italian seasoning

Cut fillets into serving-size pieces. Lay in a greased 9- by 13-inch baking pan. Brush with butter. Combine remaining ingredients in a small bowl. Sprinkle over fillets. Bake, uncovered, at 425 degrees for 10 minutes or until fish flakes easily with a fork. Serve with melted butter or tartar sauce on the side.

Pan-Fried Smelt

2 pounds smelt, cleaned
1/2 cup all-purpose flour
1/4 teaspoon garlic powder
1 teaspoon salt
1/4 teaspoon pepper
2 eggs
2 tablespoons water
1/2 cup dry bread crumbs
1/2 cup vegetable oil
2 tablespoons butter or margarine

Combine flour, garlic powder, salt and pepper in a shallow bowl. In a separate bowl, beat eggs; add water and beat again to blend. Place bread crumbs in another shallow bowl. Place a wire rack over a sheet of wax paper. Dip each fish in flour, then into the eggs, and then in the bread crumbs. Place coated fish on rack and let dry 30 minutes.

Heat oil and butter in a large skillet over medium heat. Fry fish a few at a time, turning after they have fried for several minutes. Continue to fry, turning again, until fish flakes easily with a fork. Remove fish with a slotted spoon to a pan lined with paper toweling. Cover and keep warm. Continue frying fish until all are cooked. Serve with lemon wedges and tartar sauce.

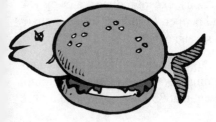

Flake leftover fish, mix with seasonings and mayonnaise to make a quick fish spread for a sandwich.

Parmesan Perch

1 pound perch fillets
3 tablespoons green onions, minced
2 tomatoes, seeded and cubed
1/4 teaspoon basil
1/2 teaspoon sugar
1/4 cup butter
Salt and pepper
Parmesan cheese

Arrange fillets in a single layer in a buttered shallow baking pan. Sprinkle with green onions, salt and pepper. Mix tomatoes with basil and sugar in a bowl; spoon over fillets. Melt butter and drizzle over fillets. Sprinkle Parmesan cheese on top. Bake at 425 degrees for 10 minutes or until fish flakes easily. Serve with cottage fries and coleslaw.

Variation: Substitute crappie or bluegill.

Perch and Potato Bake

2 pounds perch fillets
1 package (5.25-ounce) instant potatoes
1 package (10-ounce) frozen chopped spinach, cooked and well drained
1/2 cup sour cream or sour half-and-half
1/8 teaspoon pepper
1/4 cup milk
1/2 cup herb seasoned stuffing mix, crushed
2 tablespoons butter or margarine, melted
Lemon slices

Prepare potatoes according to package directions, except reduce water by 1/4 cup. Stir in spinach, sour Half-and-Half, and pepper. Lightly grease a 2-quart baking dish. Turn potato mixture into dish; spread evenly.

Pour milk into a shallow bowl. If fillets are large, cut into smaller pieces. Dip one side of each fillet in milk, then into stuffing mix. Lay on top of potato mixture. Drizzle with melted butter. Bake uncovered at 350 degrees for 30 to 35 minutes, or until fish flakes easily.

Variation: Substitute walleye, northern, or crappie.

Prairie River Trout

A simple, delicious dish and a good shore lunch recipe

Trout, cleaned
1 tablespoon minced parsley
1 cup fresh mushrooms, sliced
1 cup butter
Dash of nutmeg
Salt and paprika
Juice of 1 lemon

Lay trout in a large enough shallow baking pan. In a small saucepan, melt butter, and then add the mushrooms, parsley, lemon juice, salt, pepper and nutmeg. Stir to blend ingredients. Pour mixture over trout. Bake at 325 degrees for 15 to 20 minutes, or until fish flakes easily.

Shore lunch method:

Melt butter in a large cast iron skillet. Place trout in skillet and add remaining ingredients. Fry over medium heat until fish flakes easily and liquid has reduced in volume.

Serve with tangy coleslaw and hash-browned potatoes.

Rice and Fish Casserole

2-1/2 tablespoons butter
1 cup onion, finely chopped
1 cup celery, finely chopped
1/2 cup green pepper, finely chopped
2 small cloves garlic, minced
1 can (28-ounce) Italian-style tomato sauce
1/2 teaspoon basil
1/2 teaspoon oregano
3 cups cooked long grain rice
1-1/2 pounds northern pike or walleye fillets
2 cups Monterey Jack, shredded

Melt butter in skillet; sauté onion, celery, green pepper, and garlic. Add tomato sauce, basil, oregano, and salt and pepper to taste. Mix well to blend ingredients. Spray a 9- by 13-inch baking dish with cooking spray. Layer rice and fish fillets in dish. Pour sauce over fish and sprinkle with cheese. Bake in a 350-degree oven for 45 to 50 minutes or until fish flakes easily.

Rich, Cheesy Oven-Fried Perch

2 pounds perch fillets
1/2 cup milk
2 teaspoons salt
1 can french-fried onions
1/2 cup seasoned bread crumbs
2 tablespoons fresh parsley, chopped
3 tablespoons melted butter or margarine
1-1/2 tablespoons lemon juice
Parmesan cheese

Combine milk and salt in a shallow bowl. In another bowl, crush onions and combine with bread crumbs and parsley. Spray a baking sheet with nonstick cooking spray.

Dip perch fillets in milk. Because perch fillets are thin, put two fillets together, sandwich fashion, and roll in crumb mixture. Place on cookie sheet. Sprinkle any remaining crumb mixture over top of fish. Melt butter, add lemon juice, and drizzle over all the fillets. Lightly sprinkle Parmesan cheese over fillets. Bake at 375 degrees for 10 to 15 minutes or until fish flakes easily.

Variation: Substitute walleye or northern pike fillets. However, these fillets generally are thicker and should not be assembled sandwich fashion. Remainder of recipe stays the same.

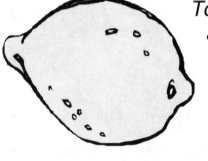

To make fish firm and white, add a little lemon juice to water while cooking.

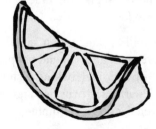

Rosemary-Marinated Salmon

Broiled, grilled, or baked, this makes for good eating

Salmon steaks cut 3/4 inch thick
4 tablespoons white wine vinegar
2 tablespoons water
2 tablespoons olive oil
4 green onions, sliced thin
3 teaspoons fresh rosemary, minced, or 3/4 teaspoon dried rosemary crushed
1 small garlic clove, finely minced
1 teaspoon fresh parsley, minced, or 1/2 teaspoon dried parsley flakes
1 tablespoon white wine
1/8 teaspoon Worcestershire sauce
1/8 teaspoon salt
Dash pepper

With the exception of the salmon, combine all ingredients in a shallow container or plastic zip-top bag. Place fish steaks in marinade; cover container. If using plastic bag, lay steaks flat in bag and seal. Turn steaks in marinade at least once. Marinate in refrigerator for 2 hours. Remove fish, reserving marinade. With any one of the cooking methods below, cook until fish begins to flake easily when tested with a fork. Cooking times are approximate. Don't overcook, or fish will become dry.

Broil: Lay fish on broiler pan. Broil 4 inches from heat source for 6 to 9 minutes. Brush steak tops with reserved marinade.

Grill: Coals should be at a medium heat. Use a wire fish basket to grill steaks. Grill fish over coals for approximately 5 to 7 minutes, turning and grilling both sides. Brush steaks with reserved marinade.

Bake: Lay steaks in a shallow pan. A cookie sheet with sides will work well. Bake at 350 degrees for 6 to 10 minutes. Brush steaks with reserved marinade.

Sally's Pickled Northern Pike

2 quarts of fish cut into bite size pieces
1 cup canning salt
1 gallon vinegar
3 cups white sugar
3 cups white port wine
6 cups vinegar
24 peppercorns
36 whole allspice
5 large onions, sliced thin

Place fish in a non-metal bowl. Mix 1 cup canning salt into fish; cover fish with water. Stir. Place lid or plate over bowl and refrigerate for 24 hours. After 24 hours, rinse fish in colander; return to bowl. Cover fish with white vinegar. Stir. Place lid or plate over bowl and refrigerate for another 24 hours.

To make brine, combine sugar, port wine, vinegar, peppercorns, and allspice in a saucepan. Bring to a boil. Remove from heat and cool completely.

Rinse fish well to remove salt water; drain in a colander. Use either two quart or four pint jars for assembling fish into jar. Begin layering with onion slices on bottom of jars, then a layer of fish. Continue to alternate layers, ending with onion on top. Pour cooled brine into jars. Use a table knife and slide it down inside of jar. This will let brine seep to the bottom of the jar. Seal jars and store in refrigerator. Let stand for at least 2 weeks prior to eating.

Scott & Sally Willman, Three Lakes, WI

Salmon Loaf with White Sauce

2 cups flaked salmon, from leftovers
1 tablespoon butter or margarine
1/4 cup minced onion
1 cup fine bread crumbs
1 cup warm milk
2 eggs, beaten
Salt and pepper

Remove any remaining skin and bones from leftover salmon. In a bowl, flake salmon to a fine texture with a fork. Heat milk and butter in a saucepan until butter melts. Remove and cool. Stir the salmon, breadcrumbs, eggs, salt and pepper into milk.

Spoon mixture into a buttered casserole or bread pan. Bake at 350 degrees for about one hour, or until center is firm. Prepare White Sauce recipe (See p. 239). Turn out loaf onto a platter and pour White Sauce over the top. Serve with mashed potatoes or pasta.

Salmon with Oriental Cranberry Sauce

A taste sensation

2 pounds salmon fillets
1-1/2 cups canned whole cranberry sauce
1/3 cup honey
1/3 cup soy sauce
2 cloves garlic, minced
1/4 teaspoon black pepper

Remove skin from salmon fillets. Place fillets in a lightly greased baking dish. In a bowl, combine cranberry sauce, honey, soy sauce, garlic and pepper. Spread sauce over fillets covering completely. Reserve some of the sauce for serving with salmon. Bake in a 375-degree oven for 30 minutes or until salmon flakes easily at its thickest part. Heat reserved sauce to serve along with cooked salmon.

Saucy Foiled Fillets

2 pounds walleye, bass, or northern fillets or steaks
Seasoned salt
Pepper
1/2 green pepper, seeded and cut into squares
1/2 red or yellow pepper, seeded and cut into squares
1 medium onion, sliced
12 tablespoons barbecue sauce, tomato ketchup or tomato sauce
3 tablespoons butter or margarine
4 tablespoons shredded Parmesan cheese

Divide fish into 4 equal portions. Place each portion on a square of heavy-duty foil. Lightly season fillets with seasoned salt and pepper. Top each portion with peppers, onion, and 3 tablespoons of barbecue sauce. Dot each portion with butter. Sprinkle each with Parmesan cheese. Seal packets tightly.

Bake: Bake in oven at 325 degrees. Set packets on cookie sheet to catch juices.

Grill: Place packets over a medium-hot fire. Cook 15 to 20 minutes or until fish flakes.

NEVER refreeze fish after being thawed.

Savory Fish Stew

Panfish or northern pike are excellent in this dish

2 pounds boneless northern fillets cut in large chunks
1 whole bay leaf
2 medium onions, chopped
4 potatoes, peeled and diced
3 carrots, peeled and diced
2 ribs celery, diced
2 teaspoons dried parsley
1/2 teaspoon dried sweet basil
2 tablespoons butter or margarine
1 can (10-3/4-ounce) cream of celery soup
Salt and pepper
1/4 to 1/2 cup milk

Place fish and bay leaf in a kettle. Barely cover fish with water; simmer for 5 minutes or until meat is firm. Remove fish chunks with a slotted spoon to a container. Reserve liquid. Remove bay leaf; discard. Cool fish; check for any bones and remove.

In a separate kettle, add all vegetables, parsley, basil and butter. Cover vegetables with water. Simmer vegetables until tender. Blend in soup and 1/2 cup reserved liquid. Add fish chunks; stir gently. Season with salt and pepper. Just before serving, add milk until stew reaches desired consistency. Do not boil.

Scalloped Potatoes & Fish Packets

2 pounds walleye, bass, or northern, fillets or steaks
Pepper
4 large potatoes, sliced
1 large onion, sliced
Seasoned salt
1 can (4-ounce) mushrooms, drained and chopped
4 tablespoons butter or margarine
4 tablespoons mild Cheddar cheese, shredded

Spray 4 squares of heavy-duty foil with seasoned cooking spray. Divide potatoes and fish into 4 equal portions. Place each portion on a square of heavy-duty foil. Lightly season with seasoned salt and pepper. Top each portion with onions and mushrooms. Dot each portion with butter. Sprinkle each with Cheddar cheese. Seal packets tightly. Bake or grill. Cook 20 to 30 minutes or until potatoes are tender and fish flakes easily.

Bake: Have oven at 325 degrees. Set packets on cookie sheet to contain juices.

Grill: Lay packets over a medium-hot fire.

Shore Lunch Walleye

Great for a quick shore lunch or fast fish fry

6 to 10 walleye fillets (medium size)
1/2 cup Bisquick
1/4 teaspoon salt
1/4 teaspoon pepper
2 tablespoons olive oil
1/4 to 1/2 cup diced onions (use more if desired)

Combine the Bisquick, salt and pepper in a plastic zip-top bag and shake to mix ingredients. Add several walleye fillets and shake to coat fish. Remove and set aside. Continue until all fillets are coated.

Heat olive oil in a skillet or electric fry pan until hot. Lay fillets in skillet and brown on one side for about 4 minutes. Add onions; turn the fillets. Continue to brown second side. Remove fillets when golden brown. To serve, spoon onions over top of fillets.

Skillet Walleye Fry

A good way to prepare your "catch of the day"

4 to 6 walleye fillets
2/3 cup yellow cornmeal
1/4 cup all-purpose flour
2 teaspoons seasoned salt
1 teaspoon dried parsley
2/3 cup evaporated milk
2 to 3 tablespoons vegetable oil

Combine cornmeal, flour, seasoned salt, and parsley in a shallow bowl. Pour evaporated milk into a bowl. Dip fillets in milk; coat with cornmeal mixture. Heat 2 tablespoons oil in a large skillet over medium-hot heat. Cook fillets in oil until golden brown on both sides and fish flakes easily. Add more vegetable oil as needed. Drain fillets on paper toweling before serving. Serve with Zesty Fish Sauce (see p. 254) or Spicy Tomato Sauce (see p. 252).

Smoked Canned Salmon

1 large salmon, dressed, skinned

Cut fish into 1 to 1-1/2 inch chunks.

Brine: In a large non-metal bowl or container, place a layer of fish and then sprinkle a generous amount of coarse, ground salt or rock salt over fish. Next layer, sprinkle brown sugar on top of salt. Repeat layers until all fish is used, ending with the brown sugar layer. Completely cover fish with cool water to soak. Place in refrigerator for 12 to 24 hours. Remove salmon from brine and drain.

Smoke: Have the smoker at 100 degrees to 120 degrees using your favorite wood. Place brined salmon on rack. Smoke for 4 hours at the given temperature. If your temperature is at 90 degrees, smoke for 8 hours. Remove from smoker.

Can: Fill pint size glass canning jars with smoked fish and seal. Do not fill jars with any liquid. Salmon will make its own liquid during processing. Place in pressure cooker. Cover, set pressure at 10 pounds. When control jiggles, cook 110 minutes. Remove cooker from heat and cool down completely. Remove jars; cool down and let seal. Check each jar to make sure it is properly sealed. Store until ready to eat and enjoy with your favorite crackers.

Note: Always read and follow manufacturer's instructions when processing with a pressure cooker.

Smoked Lake Superior Coho

Recipe makes enough for three Lake Superior Cohos, 20"- 26"

1 gallon water
1 cup canning salt
1 cup brown sugar
2 to 3 bay leaves, crushed
4 fluid ounces liquid smoke
1 teaspoon black pepper
1 teaspoon chili powder

Fillet salmon, leaving skin on. Wipe skin side well with paper toweling to remove any slime, prior to brining. This helps eliminate any fishy taste. Add all brining ingredients in a large bowl; mix to dissolve salt and sugar. Place fish in brine; soak 24 hours.

Use a Weber charcoal grill to smoke fish. Directions are as follow:

• Use two grill grates. To separate grates, use four crunched pop cans or 2 bricks, or whatever to keep grates 1 to 2 inches apart.

• Cover bottom grate with aluminum foil. Poke holes through foil so smoke can come through to top grate.

• Start grill with charcoal in a medium pile. When coals are gray, mix in soaked maple or apple wood chunks on top of coals. Size of wood to use is about 2-by 2-by 1-inch. Not too big or too small.

• Turn down vents on grill to allow for minimal airflow. Grill is ready when the cover is warm to the hand, but not so hot you cannot keep your hand on it. Reduce airflow if too hot; increase airflow if too cool.

• Spray top grate thoroughly with non-stick cooking spray. Lay fish skin side down on top grate. Smoke for 2 to 3 hours.

• After an hour or two you may need to stir coals. Continue to check temperature to maintain an even heat.

• Remove smoked fish; cool, and enjoy.

Note: This recipe will also work well with any other salmon or trout.

South of the Border Walleye

1-1/2 to 2 pounds walleye fillets
Salt and pepper
3 tablespoons butter or margarine, melted
Prepared mild to hot tomato salsa

Cut fillets into serving size portions. Sprinkle both sides with salt and pepper. Lightly grease broiler pan. Lay fish on it. Brush fish with melted butter. Have broiler pan 2 to 4 inches from source of heat. Broil 5 to 8 minutes or until fish flakes easily with a fork. Remove from under broiler; spread prepared salsa over top of fish. Return to broiler for 1 to 2 minutes to heat salsa topping.

Stir-Fry Northern Pike

1 pound northern pike fillets, cubed
2 tablespoons peanut oil
1/2 green pepper, chopped
1/2 onion, chopped
3 stalks celery, sliced
3 stalks broccoli stems, peeled and sliced
1 package frozen snow peas
1 can (8-ounce) sliced water chestnuts, drained
Salt and pepper
Dash of ground ginger
Soy sauce, to taste
Hot cooked rice

Preheat a wok or large skillet. Coat with peanut oil. Add all vegetables; stir-fry just until tender. Season with salt, pepper, ginger, and soy sauce. Push vegetables to side of the pan. Add cubed fish and fry quickly until flaky, about 5 minutes. Adjust seasonings to taste. Serve over cooked rice.

Note: Add more oil throughout stir-frying, if needed

Variation: Use a packaged stir-fry seasoning mix; follow directions on packet. Add to ingredients and mix to blend flavor.

Stuffed Rolled Fillets

Fish fillets
5 tablespoons butter or margarine
1/2 cup fresh mushrooms, chopped, divided
1/2 cup green onions, finely chopped
4 slices firm white bread, crumbled
1 large egg
1/2 cup water
1/2 cup white wine
1 medium lime or 2 tablespoons fresh lime juice
1 tablespoon all-purpose flour
1/2 cup half-and-half
Salt and pepper

Melt 2 tablespoons butter in a medium size saucepan. Sauté onions for 2 minutes, stirring occasionally. Add 1/4 cup mushrooms; sauté one minute. Stir in bread crumbs. Remove pan from heat; cool mixture. Stir in egg until well mixed.

Bring water and wine to boiling, in a large skillet over medium heat. On each fillet, lay stuffing crosswise, dividing mixture evenly on each fillet. Start at the thin end of the fillet and roll up fish around stuffing. If necessary, secure with toothpicks to hold in place. Lay rolls seam side down in skillet with water and wine. Reduce heat to simmer. Cover, and cook for 10 to 15 minutes or until fish is firm and white. Do not overcook or boil, or fish will fall apart.

Remove fish with a slotted spoon to a warm serving dish. Cover and keep warm. Strain 1/2 cup cooking liquid from skillet; discard remainder. Clean skillet with paper toweling. In same skillet, melt 3 tablespoons butter over medium heat. Add remaining 1/4 cup mushrooms; sauté 5 minutes or until golden brown. Add lime juice and stir. Remove mushrooms from skillet; spread over fish rolls. Stir flour into mushroom liquid remaining in skillet. Gradually stir in strained 1/2 cup cooking liquid and half-and-half. Cook sauce, stirring constantly, until thickened. Salt and pepper as needed to taste. Spoon sauce over fish rolls and serve.

Succulent Trout Almondine

6 (12-ounce) trout fillets
3 tablespoons butter
2/3 cups sliced almonds, toasted
1/2 cup milk
1 egg
1/2 teaspoon almond extract
1/2 teaspoon hot sauce
1 cup all-purpose flour
1 teaspoon salt
1/2 teaspoon pepper
2 cups fresh bread crumbs

Melt butter in a large skillet over low heat; add almonds. Sauté almonds until golden. Remove from skillet; drain on paper toweling. Wipe skillet clean.

Blend together milk, egg, almond extract, and hot sauce in a shallow dish. Beat until frothy. Combine flour, salt, and pepper in a shallow bowl. Coat fillets with flour mixture; dip in egg mixture. Roll fillets in bread crumbs.

Pour oil into skillet to a depth of 1/4 inch; heat to 375 degrees. Fry trout on each side for 3 to 4 minutes or until golden. Sprinkle toasted almonds over trout before serving.

Sweet-Sour Crappies

Simple and easy

1 to 2 pounds crappie fillets
1-1/2 cups bottled sweet-and-sour dressing
Salt and pepper
2 tablespoons butter or margarine, melted

Marinate crappies in sweet-and-sour dressing for 45 minutes. Remove fillets from marinade. Lay on broiler pan; lightly salt and pepper. Drizzle melted butter over fillets. Place broiler pan 4 inches from heat source. Broil 4 minutes on one side; turn and broil second side until fish flakes easily.

Tasty Vegetable Fish Soup

1 quart water
1 medium to large rutabaga, peeled and diced
1 quart potatoes, peeled and diced
2 teaspoons salt
1 large onion, chopped fine
1 pound fish (walleye, northern pike, crappies) small chunks
1 tablespoon lemon juice
1 tablespoon all-purpose flour
1-1/2 cups half-and-half or whole milk
2 tablespoons butter or margarine
Fresh parsley, chopped fine

In a large kettle, cook rutabaga in one quart of water until tender. Add in potatoes, salt, and onion. Simmer 15 minutes. Add fish chunks and lemon juice; continue to simmer mixture for an additional 10 to 15 minutes.

Mix flour and milk with a wire whisk or fork. Slowly pour into soup, stirring to mix. Simmer for 5 minutes. If soup becomes too thick, thin by adding more half-and-half or milk until desired consistency.

Teriyaki-Style Salmon Steaks

1 cup teriyaki sauce
1 tablespoon peanut oil
3 tablespoons green onions, minced fine
3 tablespoons dried parsley
1 garlic clove, crushed
1/2 teaspoon coarse black pepper
6 salmon steaks

Combine first 6 ingredients in a bowl. Add salmon steaks. Marinate for 2 hours; turning steaks every 15 to 20 minutes.

Heat grill to medium-high temperature. Spray a wire grill basket with cooking spray. Remove steaks from marinade; lay in basket. Grill for 5 minutes on one side; turn and grill other side. Baste with marinade during grilling. Grill until fish flakes easily.

Trout with Lemon Rice Stuffing

3 or 4 pounds dressed trout
1-1/2 teaspoons salt
2 tablespoons melted butter

Clean, wash, and dry trout with paper toweling. Sprinkle cavity with a little salt. Stuff loosely with prepared stuffing. Close cavity with skewers or toothpicks. Lay trout on a well-greased pan. Brush with some of the melted butter. Bake in a 350-degree oven for approximately 40 to 60 minutes, or until trout flakes easily. Baste occasionally with butter during baking. Remove skewers before serving.

Lemon Rice Stuffing:

3/4 cup celery, chopped
1/2 cup onion, chopped
1/4 cup butter, melted
1-1/3 cups water
1 teaspoon paprika
1/8 teaspoon poultry seasoning
2 tablespoons grated lemon rind
1-1/2 cups precooked rice
1/3 cup sour cream
1/4 cup lemon, peeled, diced
1 teaspoon salt

In a large skillet, sauté celery and onion in butter until tender. Add water, lemon rind, salt, paprika, and poultry seasoning. Bring contents to a boil. Reduce heat; add cooked rice. Stir to moisten. Cover and remove from heat. Let stand 5 to 10 minutes or until liquid is absorbed. Stir in sour cream and lemon. Use stuffing in recipe.

Variation: Substitute northern or whitefish.

Walleye Au Gratin

6 to 8 walleye fillets
6 tablespoons mayonnaise
1 cup green onions, chopped fine
1/2 cup Parmesan cheese, grated
1/3 cup butter or margarine
1/2 teaspoon Worcestershire sauce
2 to 3 drops Tabasco sauce
1/2 cup Cheddar cheese, shredded

Combine mayonnaise, onions, Parmesan cheese, butter, Worcestershire sauce, and Tabasco sauce in a bowl. Mix thoroughly.

Poach fillets in a skillet of simmering water for 4 minutes. Remove with a slotted spatula; drain off as much liquid as possible. Place fillets in a single layer, in a shallow baking pan. Spoon onion mixture over each fillet. Sprinkle Cheddar cheese over tops of fillets. Broil 2 to 3 minutes or until cheese is lightly browned and fish flakes easily with a fork.

Walleye Sour Cream Bake

4 to 6 walleye fillets
Juice of 2 lemons
4 tablespoons butter, melted
Salt and pepper
3/4 cup sour cream
1 cup green onions, sliced thin
1 green pepper, seeded, sliced thin

Arrange fillets in a buttered 9- by 13-inch baking pan. Drizzle lemon juice and butter over walleye fillets. Lightly salt and pepper. Bake at 350 degrees for 10 minutes. Remove from oven. Spread sour cream over fillets. Top with onions and green peppers. Bake for 10 more minutes, or until fish flakes easily.

Wine-Sauce Walleye

4 to 6 walleye fillets
2 tablespoons butter or margarine, melted
1 can (15-ounce) tomato sauce
1/2 cup dry red wine
1/2 cup butter or margarine
2 tablespoons lemon juice
2 tablespoons green onion, chopped
1 teaspoon sugar
1 teaspoon dried salad herbs
2 to 4 drops hot pepper sauce
2 to 3 tablespoons olive oil

In a small saucepan, combine tomato sauce, wine, butter, lemon juice, onion, sugar, salad herbs, and hot pepper sauce. Simmer, uncovered, for 10 minutes.

Arrange walleye fillets on lightly sprayed broiler rack. Drizzle butter over fillets. Place under broiler 4 to 5 inches from heat source. Broil until fish flakes easily with a fork. Brush fish with some of the sauce during broiling. Remove fish to warm serving dish. Serve remaining sauce separately.

If the fish has been cooked without breading, flake it up and add to a chowder recipe.

Wonton Walleye

Walleye fillets (enough to make 1 cup flaked, cooked meat)
1 cup cabbage, finely shredded
1/8 cup carrot, finely shredded
1 tablespoon fresh parsley, minced
4 green onions, diced
1 tablespoon hoisin sauce
1 teaspoon sesame oil
36 wonton wrappers
Peanut oil

Place walleye fillets in a skillet along with water to cover. Add a dash of salt. Bring to a simmer and simmer until fillets turn white. Remove; cool and shred into fine pieces.

Stir together fish meat and next 6 ingredients. Spoon 1 teaspoon of this mixture in center of each wonton wrapper. Moisten wonton edges with water. Bring corners together, pressing to seal.

Heat peanut oil in a Dutch oven, small deep fryer, or electric skillet to 375 degrees. Fry wontons in batches until golden on all sides. Remove and drain on wire racks over paper towels. Serve immediately with Honey Mustard Sauce (see p. 248) or Hoisin Peanut Dipping Sauce (see p. 247).

Yummy Buttered Lake Perch

A lightly breaded and golden brown taste sensation for this lake fish

2 to 3 pounds lake perch
2/3 cup all-purpose flour
1/3 cup cornmeal or dry bread crumbs
1/2 teaspoon paprika
1/4 teaspoon onion powder
1/8 teaspoon garlic powder
Salt and pepper
Vegetable oil
1 stick butter or margarine
2 eggs, beaten

In a bowl, combine flour, cornmeal or bread crumbs, paprika, onion and garlic powders, and salt and pepper.

Heat 6 tablespoons of vegetable oil in a skillet or electric frying pan to 375 degrees; add 2 tablespoons butter. In a separate bowl, beat eggs; dip fillets in the eggs, then coat with flour mixture. Shake off excess. Fry each side until golden brown. Remove fish and keep warm, until all fish are cooked. Serve with home-made tartar sauce and lemon wedges.

To eliminate a fishy taste, cover fish with milk and soak for approximately one hour before cooking.

OTHER
SAVORY
DISHES

Wild Rice

A high-fiber carbohydrate, wild rice is low in calories and fat, yet high in nutritional value. One-half cup of cooked wild rice has only 70 calories. It is excellent served any number of ways, as an accompaniment to wild game, as a cereal, in a casserole, or as a cold salad. It is also a nutritious substitute for potatoes or white rice.

A rule-of-thumb: One cup of raw wild rice increases to about three to four cups when cooked. Keep in mind that the cooked grain will open more when added as an ingredient in a casserole or soup. Over-cooking the rice will produce a "rolled back" or mushy look to the kernel.

It is a good idea to have precooked wild rice on hand. Prepare a batch, drain well, and keep in a tightly covered container or plastic zip-top bag in the refrigerator. Wild rice will keep in the refrigerator for up to a week or can be frozen for longer storage. When freezing cooked wild rice, package amount normally used in a recipe into individual containers or plastic bags. Label with date and amount enclosed. Frozen, it will keep up to six months. To use when frozen, place in hot water; stir and then drain, removing as much water as possible. The rice is now ready for use.

Basic Recipe for Wild Rice

1 cup uncooked wild rice
3 to 4 cups water (or chicken or beef broth)
1 teaspoon salt (omit salt if using broth)

Stovetop method: Rinse rice under cold, running water and drain. Place in saucepan with water and salt, if desired. Bring to a boil, reduce heat to a simmer and cover. Simmer for about 30 to 45 minutes or until most of the grains just begin to puff open. Remove saucepan, drain, and the wild rice is ready for use.

Oven method: Place rice in a strainer. Rinse under cold, running water, drain, then place in an ovenproof casserole dish. Add just enough water to cover the rice. Cover the casserole and bake at 350 degrees for about 1-1/2 hours or until liquid has been absorbed.

Almond Wild Rice Stuffing

Serve as a stuffing or side dish

1/2 cup butter or margarine
1/2 cup green onions, chopped fine
4 cups cooked wild rice
1/2 cup slivered almonds
1 teaspoon poultry seasoning
Salt and/or pepper, as needed

Melt butter in a skillet; sauté onions until tender. Mix in cooked wild rice, almonds, and seasonings. Serve or use to stuff bird.

Cabinhaus Wild Rice Stuffing

Basic stuffing recipe for game birds or ducks

1 to 1-1/2 cups uncooked wild rice
5 cups water
1/4 cup butter or margarine
1/2 cup onion, chopped
1/2 cup celery, finely chopped
1 can (10-3/4-ounce) cream of mushroom soup
1/4 cup milk
1 tablespoon instant chicken bouillon granules
1/4 to 1/2 teaspoon poultry seasoning
Salt and pepper, to taste

Combine water and rice in a saucepan; cook until rice has just opened. Drain, rinse and set aside.

In a large skillet, sauté onions and celery in butter until tender-crisp. Mix vegetables in with the wild rice. Combine soup, milk, and bouillon granules, stirring to blend. Pour over wild rice. Season with poultry seasoning, salt and pepper. Thoroughly mix all ingredients. Before roasting, place some stuffing on top of breasts to keep meat moist; roast according to recipe.

To judge the stages of doneness, remove small spoonfuls during final cooking to see how you like it.

Camp 6 Wild Rice Mushroom Soup

1/2 pound bacon
2 medium onions, chopped
4 ribs celery, sliced
2 cans (8-ounce) sliced mushrooms, drained
1/2 cup carrots, peeled and grated
1/4 cup all-purpose flour
1 tablespoon instant chicken bouillon granules
2 cans (14-1/2-ounce) chicken broth
2 cans (10-3/4-ounce) cream of mushroom soup
1/2 teaspoon poultry seasoning
1 to 2 cups half-and-half or milk
2 cups cooked wild rice
Salt and pepper to taste

Over medium heat, sauté bacon in a Dutch oven or large kettle until crisp. Remove; set aside. Sauté onion, celery, mushrooms, and carrots in the bacon drippings until tender crisp. Stir in flour, coating all vegetables. Add chicken granules, chicken broth, 2 cans soup, and poultry seasoning. Cook, stirring until soup thickens and bubbles. Stir in 1 cup half-and-half to mixture; mix well. Stir in part or all of the wild rice, depending on how thick or thin a soup is desired. Salt and pepper to taste. If soup becomes too thick, add remaining half-and-half. Cook until soup bubbles. Serve bowls of soup with crumbled bacon on top.

Company Wild Rice Hot Dish

1 cup uncooked wild rice
1 pound pork sausage or pork links
1 to 2 tablespoons butter or margarine
1 cup green onions, chopped
1 green pepper, chopped
1 cup celery, chopped
1/2 pound fresh mushrooms, sliced
1 can (10-3/4-ounce) cream of mushroom soup
1 can (6-ounce) evaporated milk

Cook wild rice until it just begins to open. It should be slightly crunchy, not mushy. Drain, rinse, and set aside.

While rice is cooking, cook pork sausage or pork links in a skillet, until done. Drain off grease. Cool, and then crumble sausage. If using pork links, cut into small 1/4- to 1/2-inch pieces. Set aside. Wipe skillet out with paper toweling. Melt butter in skillet; sauté onions, pepper, celery, and mushrooms until tender.

Spray casserole dish with a cooking spray. In a small bowl, mix soup and evaporated milk. Place cooked wild rice, sautéed vegetables, and crumbled sausage into casserole dish. Add soup mixture; mix all ingredients. Bake at 350 degrees for 30 to 45 minutes.

Variation: Substitute venison hamburger or cooked, cubed pheasant.

Creamy Potato Wild Rice Soup

A delicious chill chaser on a cold day

2 cups cooked wild rice
1 large onion, chopped fine
1 cup celery, chopped fine
1/2 cup carrot, peeled and diced
1/3 cup all-purpose flour
1 teaspoon salt
1/4 teaspoon pepper
4 cups milk divided
2 cans (10-3/4-ounce) cream of potato soup
Parsley

Melt butter in a large saucepan; add onions, celery, and carrot. Cover; cook 5 minutes until tender, but not browned. Stir flour, salt and pepper into vegetables. Remove from heat; add 2 cups milk, stirring until flour is well blended. Return to low heat. Cook, stirring constantly, until soup thickens. Add in both cans of soup, blending well. Add cooked wild rice; simmer a few minutes to blend flavors. If soup becomes too thick, add remaining milk, 1 cup at a time, until desired consistency. Serve hot, garnished with a small parsley sprig.

Harvest Casserole with Wild Rice

1 cup uncooked wild rice
2 tablespoons vegetable oil
1 pound venison hamburger
1 medium onion, chopped
1 cup celery, chopped
1 medium green pepper, seeded and chopped
1 cup carrots, peeled and diced
1 cup potatoes, peeled and cubed
1 cup grated Cheddar cheese
1 can (10-3/4-ounce) cream of chicken soup
1 can (10-3/4-ounce) cream of mushroom soup
Salt and pepper

Heat oil in large skillet; brown venison hamburger. Add onion, celery, and green pepper; cook until just tender. Drain off any excess drippings. Add in uncooked wild rice, carrots, potatoes, cheese, and both soups. Mix well. Pour mixture into a greased 3-quart casserole dish. Cover. Bake at 325 degrees for 1-1/2 hours or until rice has opened.

Herbed Wild Rice Stuffing

1 cup uncooked wild rice
4 cups chicken broth
1 cup celery, diced
1/4 cup onion, minced
1/2 cup melted butter or margarine
1 can (4-ounce) mushrooms, undrained
1/2 teaspoon marjoram leaves
1/4 teaspoon oregano leaves
1/4 teaspoon thyme leaves
1 teaspoon seasoned salt
1/4 teaspoon pepper
Salt to taste

Wash wild rice. Bring chicken broth to a boil; add wild rice and bring back to a boil again. Reduce heat, cover, and simmer for 30 to 45 minutes or until rice has opened. Stir with a fork ocassionally. All of the chicken broth should be absorbed.

Sauté celery and onion in the butter until tender, but not browned. Drain mushrooms, reserving 2 tablespoons of the liquid. Add mushrooms, 2 tablespoons liquid, and celery and onion mixture to wild rice. Mix all ingredients. Check seasoning and add more to achieve desired taste. Makes approximately 6 cups. Stuff bird.

Oriental Wild Rice Casserole

3 cups cooked wild rice
2 tablespoons butter or margarine
1 medium onion, chopped
1/2 cup green pepper, diced
1/2 cup red pepper, diced
1/2 cup celery, sliced
1 tablespoon instant beef bouillon granules
1/2 to 3/4 cup water chestnuts, sliced
Soy sauce

Melt butter in a skillet and sauté onion, peppers, and celery until almost tender. Sprinkle beef bouillon granules into skillet; stir to dissolve. Add in water chestnuts. Place wild rice and vegetables in a buttered casserole dish. Stir to mix. Season with soy sauce to taste. Bake casserole in a 325-degree oven for 30 minutes or until heated through.

Rice Pilaf with Cranberries

A combination of wild and brown rice and cranberries

1/3 cup dried cranberries (craisins)
1/3 cup dry white wine
3 cups chicken broth, divided
3/4 cup green onions, minced
3/4 cup uncooked brown rice
1 cup apple cider
3/4 cup uncooked wild rice

Plump cranberries in wine for 15 minutes. Drain cranberries, reserving liquid. In a saucepan, add reserved cranberry liquid and 1-1/2 cups broth, along with brown rice and onions. Bring to a boil. Reduce heat and cover. Cook until rice is tender and most or all of liquid absorbed, about 40 minutes.

In another saucepan, add apple cider, remaining 1-1/2 cups broth, and wild rice. Bring to a boil. Reduce heat, cover, cook until rice has begun to open. Drain off excess liquid.

Combine both wild and brown rice and plumped cranberries in saucepan, mixing well. Heat and serve.

Skillet Wild Rice and Bacon

Unbelievably simple – unbelievably tasty

3 cups cooked wild rice
1/2 pound bacon, diced
1/2 cup green onions, minced
Pepper

Fry bacon in a heavy skillet. Remove bacon and set aside. Drain off drippings to a bowl. Return 4 tablespoons of drippings to skillet. Sauté onions until tender. Add in bacon and wild rice. Stir to blend ingredients. Season with pepper. Add a tablespoon of reserved drippings if needed for taste. Heat mixture and serve.

Snow Peas & Wild Rice Salad

An elegant salad to serve

1-1/2 tablespoons red wine vinegar
1/4 teaspoon salt
1/4 teaspoon fresh black pepper
1/3 cup plus 3 tablespoons olive oil (divided)
1 tablespoon Dijon-style mustard
1-1/2 tablespoons fresh lemon juice
1/2 teaspoon crushed dried rosemary
1 cup uncooked wild rice
2-1/4 cups chicken broth
1/3 cup sliced water chestnuts
1/2 red bell pepper, seeded and diced
2 tablespoons minced green onions
Salt to taste
1/3 pound snow peas, ends trimmed
1/4 pound fresh mushrooms, sliced

In small bowl, combine vinegar, salt, pepper, 1/3-cup oil, mustard, lemon juice, and rosemary. Whisk or blend with a fork. Cover; set aside.

Heat remaining 3 tablespoons olive oil in 2-quart saucepan. Add rice and chicken broth; bring to boil; reduce heat to simmer. Cover and cook until rice is tender. (Liquid should be evaporated.) Put rice in mixing bowl; add 1/4 cup of dressing, water chestnuts, red pepper, green onions, and salt and pepper to taste. Stir gently. Cover and let flavors blend 1 hour.

Steam snow peas until still slightly crisp, 4 to 8 minutes. Cut into 1-inch pieces; put in small mixing bowl. Add mushrooms and remaining dressing. Toss to distribute dressing evenly. Turn wild rice mixture into salad bowl or plate, mounding and making a well in center. Mound peas and mushrooms in the well. Serve immediately.

Spanish Wild Rice

1/2 pound bacon cut into 1 inch pieces
2 medium onions, chopped fine
1 cup celery, chopped
1 large green pepper, seeded and chopped
1/2 red pepper, seeded and chopped
1 can (28-ounce) tomatoes, undrained
1/2 teaspoon oregano
Salt and pepper
Chili powder or cayenne pepper to taste
1 cup uncooked wild rice
1 can (8-ounce) tomato sauce, as needed

Fry bacon in a skillet until crisp. Push bacon to one side of pan; sauté onions, celery, and peppers for 5 minutes. Add in tomatoes, oregano, salt and pepper, chili powder or cayenne pepper; heat through. Butter a casserole dish. Add in rice and tomato mixture; stir to mix. Cover casserole and bake at 325 degrees for 2 hours. Check casserole occasionally. If mixture begins to appear dry, stir in a little tomato sauce to moisten.

Wild Rice Almondine Bake

1 cup uncooked wild rice
1/2 cup uncooked white rice
1-1/2 cups water
1/4 cup onion, chopped
1/4 cup red pepper, chopped
1/4 cup butter, melted
2 (10-3/4-ounce) cans chicken broth
1 can (8-ounce) whole mushrooms, undrained
3 tablespoons sliced almonds

Combine all ingredients, except almonds, in an ungreased 2-quart casserole dish. Cover, bake at 350 degrees for 1 to 1-1/2 hours, or until rice is tender and liquid is absorbed. Stir mixture occasionally. Garnish with sliced almonds.

Wild Rice Asparagus Salad

1 cup uncooked rice
1 chicken bouillon cube
1 pound asparagus
2-1/2 cups turkey, cubed
1 cup pineapple bits, drained (optional)
1/2 teaspoon ginger
1/4 cup white wine vinegar
1 tablespoon balsamic vinegar or soy sauce
1 tablespoon sugar
1/3 cup oil
1/2 cup cashews

Cook wild rice in 3 cups water with chicken bouillon cube, until rice has slightly opened. Drain, rinse, and put into a large bowl.

Blanch asparagus spears, cool immediately. Cut into 1 inch pieces. Add asparagus, turkey, and pineapple to cooked wild rice. Mix together ginger, white wine vinegar, balsamic vinegar, sugar and oil. Stir until sugar is dissolved. Pour over wild rice, mix to blend dressing throughout salad. Sprinkle cashews over salad. Cover, refrigerate until time of serving.

Wild Rice Cranberry Casserole

Simple and terrific as a side dish

4 cups cooked wild rice
1/2 cup chopped fresh cranberries **or**
3/4 cup dried cranberries (craisens)
2 teaspoons fresh, snipped parsley, to taste

Combine wild rice, cranberries, and parsley in a buttered casserole dish. Cover and bake at 325 degrees for 30 minutes or until heated through.

Wild Rice Medley

An excellent accompaniment with any game dish

1-1/2 cups uncooked wild rice
5 cups water
1/4 cup butter or margarine
1/2 cup onion, chopped
1/2 cup celery, finely chopped
1/2 pound fresh mushrooms, sliced
1 tablespoon instant chicken bouillon granules
Pepper

Combine water and rice in a saucepan. Cook until rice has opened sufficiently. Drain, rinse and set aside. In a large skillet over medium heat, sauté onions, celery, and mushrooms in butter until tender-crisp. Lower heat to simmer. Stir and blend in bouillon granules to dissolve. Stir in wild rice with the vegetables. Season with pepper. Heat and serve.

Wild Rice Orange & Craisin Salad

1 cup uncooked wild rice
1 cup chopped walnuts or pecans
1 cup craisins, chopped cranberries or raisins
1 can (8-ounce) Mandarin orange sections, drained
4 sliced green onions and tops
1/4 cup olive oil
1/3 cup orange juice
1/8 teaspoon salt (or less)
1 to 2 tablespoons balsamic vinegar

Combine 3 cups chicken broth and rice in a saucepan; cook until rice has just opened. Drain, rinse, and place in a large bowl. Add in remaining ingredients; mix well. Refrigerate and serve chilled.

Note: Add chopped water chestnuts for a crunchier salad.

Wild Rice Partridge or Pheasant Salad

Dressing:
1/2 cup salad dressing
1/3 cup dairy sour cream or sour Half-and-Half
1/2 teaspoon salt
1/4 teaspoon marjoram
1/8 teaspoon pepper

Salad:
3 cups cooked wild rice, chilled
2 cups cooked patridge or pheasant, cubed
1/2 cup celery, sliced
1/2 cup red bell pepper, seeded and diced
1/4 cup green bell pepper, seeded and diced
1/4 pound fresh mushrooms, sliced
1/4 cup green onions, sliced
1/3 cup water chestnuts, sliced
1/4 to 1/2 cup toasted slivered almonds

In small bowl, combine all dressing ingredients; set aside. In large salad bowl, combine all salad ingredients. Add dressing to salad mixture. Toss gently to distribute dressing evenly. Cover, refrigerate 2 to 3 hours to blend flavors. Serve on salad plates garnished with lettuce leaves and tomato wedges.

Wild Rice Pilaf Almandine

3 tablespoons butter or margarine
1 medium onion, chopped
2 celery ribs, diced
1/4 cup carrot, peeled and diced
1/2 cup slivered almonds
1/2 cup uncooked wild rice
1 cup fresh mushrooms, chopped
1-1/2 cups beef broth

Melt butter in a large skillet over medium-high heat. Sauté onion, celery, carrots, and almonds for 3 minutes. Add wild rice and mushrooms; sauté for an additional 4 minutes. Add in beef broth to skillet. Reduce heat to simmer, cover and cook until rice has opened sufficiently.

Wild Rice Venison Medley

2 cups cooked wild rice
1 pound venison hamburger
1 tablespoon oil
1 medium onion, chopped
1 cup celery, chopped
1/2 cup carrots, sliced
1 can (14-1/2-ounce) stewed tomatoes, undrained
1/2 bag (28-ounce) hash browns
1 can (10-3/4-ounce) cream of celery soup
Shredded mild Cheddar cheese
French fried onions

Brown venison hamburger in oil with onion and celery. Drain off excess liquid. In a greased 2- or 3-quart casserole, add hamburger mixture, carrots, tomatoes, hash browns, and celery soup. Mix.

Bake in a 325-degree oven for 45 minutes. Add cheese to top of casserole, sprinkle with French fried onions. Return to oven; bake until cheese has melted.

Workday Wild Rice Casserole

Casserole takes only about one hour to prepare, bake, and serve

1 pound venison hamburger
1 tablespoon butter or vegetable oil
1 cup uncooked wild rice
1 large onion, diced
1 can (16-ounce) stewed tomatoes, undrained
1 can (10-3/4-ounce) cream of mushroom soup
6 ribs celery, chopped fine
1 can (4-ounce) sliced mushrooms, drained (optional)
1/2 teaspoon dried poultry seasoning
Salt and pepper, to taste

Brown hamburger in a skillet. Butter a 3-quart casserole dish. Mix all ingredients in casserole. Cover, bake at 325 degrees for one hour or until rice opens. If casserole becomes dry, add a little water or tomato juice to moisten.

Wild Rice Sausage Dressing

First-rate dressing for ducks, geese, and turkey, or as a side dish

1 cup uncooked wild rice
4 cups chicken or beef broth
4 tablespoons butter or margarine
1 cup celery, chopped
1 cup onion, finely chopped
1/2 pound seasoned pork sausage
1/2 to 1 teaspoon poultry seasoning
Salt and pepper

Wash wild rice, drain and place in saucepan with chicken or beef broth. Cover, simmer for 30 to 45 minutes, or until rice is opened. Drain; transfer wild rice to a bowl.

Melt butter in a skillet; sauté celery and onion until tender. Mix in with wild rice. Brown sausage in skillet. Drain off excess fat. Add sausage and seasonings to wild rice. Mix well.

Variation: Bake dressing in a buttered casserole dish or loaf pan. Cover, bake at 325 degrees for one hour. Can also be cooked in a Crock-Pot.

Don't throw out leftover wine. Freeze it in ice cube trays, and store in zip-top plastic bags for use in soups, sauces, and casseroles

Super Side Dishes

A meal wouldn't be complete without side dishes. They complement any main course, and some just naturally go together, like fish and coleslaw, turkey and dressing, mashed potatoes and gravy. When serving game and fish, remember the entrée should not be upstaged by the accompaniments. On the following pages you're sure to find the right side dish to make your game or fish dinner a memorable one.

But wait! Don't forget the dessert. To top off that scrumptious meal, how about Rhubarb Custard Pie, or for something light, Cranberry Ice?

Apple Coleslaw

A little out of the ordinary

1/4 cup mayonnaise or salad dressing
1/2 cup vanilla-flavored yogurt
1/4 teaspoon sugar
1 tablespoon milk
1/4 teaspoon ground cinnamon
3 cups green cabbage, finely shredded
1 cup red cabbage, finely shredded
2 cups apples, cored and diced
1/2 cup carrot, peeled and diced
1/4 cup green onion sliced (optional)

To make dressing, mix together mayonnaise or salad dressing, yogurt, sugar, milk, and cinnamon. In a large bowl combine cabbage, apples, carrot and onion. Pour dressing over cabbage mixture, stir mixture to coat. Cover and chill in refrigerator.

Applesauce Glazed Squash

3 small acorn squash, cut in half, seeded
Salt and pepper
Cinnamon
Nutmeg
1/4 cup butter or margarine, melted
1-1/2 cups chunky applesauce
1/2 cup firmly packed dark brown sugar

Place squash halves, cut side down, in 9- by 13-inch baking pan. Fill pan with hot water to 1/4 inch depth. Bake at 400 degrees for 30 minutes or until squash is tender. Invert squash halves; mash each squash half with a fork, leaving shell intact. Season each half with salt, pepper, cinnamon, and a dash of nutmeg. Drizzle butter over each half. Mix lightly. Top each with applesauce and brown sugar. Return to oven; bake 10 to 15 minutes longer or until brown sugar is melted.

Cabbage Slaw Jell-O

A 1950s favorite - tart flavor and crisp texture

1 package (3-ounce) lemon lime or orange-flavored Jell-O
1/8 teaspoon salt
1 cup boiling water
3/4 cup cold water
2 tablespoons cider vinegar
1/2 small head cabbage, shredded fine
1/2 cup celery, sliced fine
Mayonnaise or salad dressing

In a bowl, dissolve Jell-O and salt in boiling water. Add cold water and vinegar; mix well. Chill in refrigerator until thickened but not set, about 30 minutes. Fold in remaining ingredients. Lightly spray an 8-inch square pan with cooking spray. Pour mixture into pan. Refrigerate until firm. Spread thin layer of mayonnaise or salad dressing over top of Jell-O. Cut into squares and serve on lettuce leaves.

Can-Fried Potatoes

When time is short, canned potatoes are the answer

3 to 4 cans (14-1/2-ounce) whole canned potatoes
4 tablespoons butter
2 tablespoons chicken bouillon granules
Pepper
Dried parsley flakes

Drain potatoes. In a non-stick or electric skillet, melt butter over medium heat. Add potatoes. Sprinkle bouillon over potatoes and lightly pepper. Turn potatoes occasionally; brown to a rich golden color on all sides, about 15 to 20 minutes. Sprinkle parsley flakes over potatoes and serve.

Cauliflower Onion Bake

1-1/2 cups water
2 tablespoons butter
1 package (10-ounce) frozen cauliflower, thawed
2 packages (10-ounce) frozen onions in cream sauce
3/4 cup shredded sharp cheddar cheese
1/2 cup toasted slivered almonds
1 tablespoon parsley flakes
1/2 cup canned French fried onions, crumbled

Cut cauliflower into bite-sized pieces. In saucepan, combine water, butter, and the two packages frozen onions. Cover and bring to boiling. Reduce heat, simmer, covered, for 4 minutes, stirring occasionally. Remove from heat; stir until sauce is smooth.

Add cauliflower, shredded cheese, almonds, and parsley to creamed onions. Pour mixture into a 1-1/2 quart casserole. Bake at 350 degrees for 35 minutes or until bubbly and heated through. Top with crumbled French fried onions and bake 5 minutes more.

Celery Stuffing

1 garlic clove, minced
1 small onion, chopped fine
4 tablespoons butter or margarine
2 cups soft bread crumbs
2 tablespoons chopped thyme
4 ribs celery, chopped (use tops also)
4 tablespoons blanched, toasted almonds, chopped
Salt and pepper

Melt butter in a skillet; sauté garlic and onion until tender. Combine all ingredients in a bowl, mixing well to blend seasonings throughout mixture. Let mixture cool, before using stuffing.

Corn Bread Sausage Stuffing

1/2 cup butter or margarine
3/4 cup onions, minced
1/2 cup green peppers, minced
1/2 cup celery, minced
5 cups white bread crumbs
5 cups crumbled corn bread (made without sugar)
1 chicken bouillon cube
1/2 pound pork sausage links
1/4 teaspoon salt
1/8 teaspoon pepper
1/2 teaspoon poultry seasoning
2 eggs, beaten

Melt butter in a skillet; sauté onions, green peppers, and celery until tender. Place bread crumbs and corn bread in a bowl. Dissolve bouillon cube in 2/3 cups hot water; sprinkle over crumbs. Add sautéed vegetables. In same skillet, cook sausage until browned. To crumb mixture, add salt, pepper, poultry seasoning, eggs, sausage and drippings. Mix all ingredients to blend flavors. Stuffing is ready for use.

Cornmeal Stuffing

3 cups chicken broth
1/2 cup cornmeal
3 cups soft bread cubes
3/4 cup celery, finely diced
1 large onion, chopped
1 tablespoon poultry seasoning
1 egg, well beaten
1/8 teaspoon dried sage
Salt and pepper

Heat broth to boiling. Gradually add cornmeal, stirring constantly. Reduce heat, cook for 10 minutes. Stir occasionally. Add bread cubes, celery, onions, poultry seasoning, and egg. Season to taste with sage, salt and pepper. Mix thoroughly. Stuff cleaned cavity of bird immediately with mixture. Close cavity and bake accordingly.

Cranberry Corn Bread Stuffing

Particularly good with wild duck

1 cup cranberries, chopped
1/4 cup sugar
4 tablespoons butter or margarine
1/4 cup celery, chopped
2/3 cup cooked ham or cooked bacon, diced
3 cups white bread crumbs
1 cup corn bread crumbs
1/4 teaspoon poultry seasoning

Wash and sort through cranberries. Run cranberries through a food chopper. Place in a bowl and add sugar. Melt butter in a skillet. Sauté celery with the ham or bacon for 5 minutes. Add to cranberry mixture. Add in bread crumbs and seasoning; blend mixture. Stuffing is ready for use.

Creamy Cranberry Salad

1 package (3-ounce) cream cheese
2 cups frozen whipped dessert topping, thawed
1 can (11-ounce) mandarin orange sections, drained
1 jar (14-ounce) cranberry-orange relish
1-1/2 cups miniature marshmallows
1 can (8-3/4-ounce) crushed pineapple, drained
1/3 cup chopped walnuts

Beat cream cheese into dessert topping. Reserve a few mandarin oranges for garnish. Stir remaining ingredients into dessert topping. Chill several hours before serving. Serve on a bed of lettuce.

Fruit Dressing for Fowl

1/2 pound prunes
1/4 cup raisins
1/4 cup currants
4 large tart apples, peeled, cored and diced
1/2 cup water
2 tablespoons sugar
1/2 teaspoon salt
1/3 teaspoon cinnamon
1/4 teaspoon nutmeg
2 tablespoons butter
3 cups stale white bread, cut into tiny cubes,
Or, purchase bread cubes
1/4 teaspoon thyme

Pit the prunes, place in a pan along with raisins, currants, and apples. Add water and bring to a boil. Reduce heat, simmer until fruit is tender. Add sugar, salt, cinnamon, nutmeg, and butter. Fold in bread cubes and thyme; gently mix to blend seasonings and bread cubes.

This will make enough stuffing for two ducks, a goose, or a small turkey.

Fruity Cabbage Salad

1/2 cup whipping cream
1 tablespoon sugar
1 tablespoon lemon juice
1/4 teaspoon salt
3/4 cup mayonnaise or salad dressing
2 oranges, peeled, sectioned, and cut in half
2 medium apples, chopped
2 cups green cabbage, shredded
1 cup red cabbage, shredded
1 cup seedless grapes, cut in half

Beat whipping cream in chilled bowl until stiff. Fold in sugar, lemon juice, salt and mayonnaise. Set aside. Place all fruit and vegetables in a bowl. Stir in cream mixture. Chill and serve.

Game Bird Rice Stuffing

1-1/2 cups uncooked white or brown rice
1 onion, sliced thin
1 can (4-ounce) sliced mushrooms, drained
4 slices bacon cut into pieces
1 cup chicken broth
1/2 cup dry white wine
6 sage leaves
Salt and pepper
1 egg, beaten

Fry bacon in a skillet until crisp; remove with a slotted spoon. Fry onion and mushrooms in drippings, until onion is transparent but not browned. Add uncooked rice, cooking until it is golden. Stir often. Add in chicken broth, wine, and sage leaves. Salt and pepper mixture. Simmer until rice is tender and liquid is absorbed. Add bacon pieces and beaten egg; mix lightly.

Makes enough to stuff 4 small game birds.

German Potato Pancakes

2 large eggs
1 small onion, chopped
1 teaspoon baking powder
2 teaspoons sugar
Dash of cinnamon
3/4 teaspoon salt
1/4 teaspoon pepper
1-1/2 pounds russet potatoes, peeled and cubed
1/4 cup all-purpose flour
Applesauce

Process first 7 ingredients in a blender until smooth. Gradually add cubed potato and flour, processing until mixture thickens.

Pour about 1/4 cup batter for each pancake onto a hot, lightly greased nonstick skillet; cook over medium-high heat until each side is browned. Serve with applesauce.

German-Style Red Cabbage

3 tablespoons butter or margarine
2 large tart apples, chopped
1 medium onion, minced
1 medium head red cabbage, shredded
1/3 cup vinegar
1/2 cup firmly packed brown sugar
2 teaspoons all-purpose flour
Salt and pepper
1/3 cup dry red wine

Melt butter in a large skillet over medium-high heat. Sauté apples and onion, 5 minutes. Add cabbage and vinegar to skillet. Combine brown sugar and flour; sprinkle mixture over cabbage. Add wine to skillet. Salt and pepper to taste. Cover, reduce heat, and simmer for about 35 minutes. Stir mixture frequently.

Great-Grandma's Bohemian Dumplings

1 cup warm milk
6 dry bread rolls, pulled apart and cut up into very small pieces or use dry bread
Salt and freshly ground black pepper to taste
2 eggs, lightly beaten
Boiling salted water

Put roll pieces in a mixing bowl; pour milk over bread pieces. Let stand at least one hour. Season mixture with salt and pepper. Mix in eggs; blend well.

Form mixture into 1-1/2-inch to 2-inch balls. Drop a few at a time into boiling, salted water. Bring water back to a boil; boil dumplings for about 20 minutes. Remove dumplings with a slotted spoon draining off any water. Serve with butter or gravy as a side dish with any wild game.

Green Bean au Gratin

2 cans (14-1/2-ounce) sliced green beans, drained
2 tablespoons olive oil
1 tablespoon wine vinegar
1 tablespoon onion, minced
1 clove garlic, minced
1/8 teaspoon pepper
3 tablespoons bread crumbs
2 tablespoons grated Parmesan cheese
1 tablespoon butter or margarine, melted
Paprika

Place green beans in an ungreased casserole dish. In a bowl, blend oil, vinegar, onion, garlic, and pepper. Pour oil mixture over green beans; toss to coat beans. Mix bread crumbs, grated cheese, and butter. Sprinkle over beans. Sprinkle lightly with paprika. Bake, uncovered, in 350-degree oven for 15 to 20 minutes.

Green Beans Oriental

A perfect side dish served with game

3 cups frozen green beans
1 teaspoon salt
1/2 cups celery, sliced
1 can (4-ounce) mushroom pieces and stems, drained
1/2 large red pepper, seeded and diced
3 tablespoons oil
1 beef bouillon cube
1-1/2 tablespoons soy sauce
1 tablespoon cornstarch
1/2 cup slivered almonds

In medium saucepan, combine beans, salt and enough water to cover. Bring to a boil, cooking until tender. Drain, reserving 1 cup liquid.

In large skillet, cook celery, mushrooms, and red pepper in oil until celery is crisp-tender. Combine the reserved 1 cup liquid with bouillon cube, soy sauce, and cornstarch. Stir into mixture in skillet. Add beans. Cook, stirring until mixture thickens and begins to boil. Stir in almonds. Serve.

Lucille's Potato Dumplings

4 cups cold mashed potatoes
3 cups all-purpose flour, more or less
1 teaspoon salt
Dash pepper
1 egg, slightly beaten
Boiling salted water

Combine potatoes, flour, salt, pepper, and egg. Mix lightly. Add in more flour if mixture is too sticky. Form into 3-inch balls. Drop into rapidly boiling salted water. Cover and cook fifteen minutes. Remove with a slotted spoon, draining off any water. Serve with butter or gravy in place of potatoes.

Marinated Cooked Vegetable Salad

2 cups carrots, diced
2 cups cauliflowerets
2 cups broccoli flowerets
Water
1 can (6-ounce) ripe pitted olives, drained

Marinade:

1/4 cup lemon juice
1/2 cup vegetable oil
1 tablespoon sugar
1 teaspoon salt
1 teaspoon grated lemon rind
3/4 teaspoon dried oregano leaves
1/4 teaspoon pepper

Place carrots, cauliflowerets, and broccoli in Dutch oven. Barely cover with water. Cook vegetables until crisp-tender, about 3 to 5 minutes. Drain well. Place cooked vegetables and ripe olives in a large casserole dish or bowl.

Combine all marinade ingredients in a jar. Cover and shake well. Pour over vegetable mixture; mix well. Cover and refrigerate at least 6 hours before serving. Stir occasionally. Drain off marinade and discard before serving salad.

Mashed Potato-Stuffing Bake

A flavor-packed side dish to team with any game dish

4 cups mashed potatoes
3/4 cup celery, finely chopped
1/2 cup green onions, finely chopped
2-1/4 cups seasoned croutons
4 slices American cheese

Grease a 2-quart casserole dish. In a separate bowl, stir together mashed potatoes, celery, and onions. Stir in 2 cups croutons. Spoon into prepared casserole. Crush remaining croutons, sprinkle around edge of mixture.

Bake at 350 degrees for 35 minutes or until light golden brown. Cut cheese slices in half diagonally; arrange slices down center of potato mixture. Return to oven, bake until cheese is melted.

Potato Dumplings

1-1/2 cups biscuit mix
1/2 cup instant potato mix
2/3 cup milk
1/2 teaspoon dried parsley
All-purpose flour

Stir together biscuit mix, potato flakes, milk, and parsley until blended. Turn dough out onto a heavily floured surface; roll or pat dough to 1/4-inch thickness. Cut into 1/2-inch strips. Pinch off 1/2-inch pieces from strips. Drop, one at a time into gently boiling water. Cover; reduce heat to simmer. Stir occasionally; cook 15 minutes or until dumplings are cooked. Remove with slotted spoon to serving bowl.

Serve with melted butter drizzled over dumplings or with gravy. Salt and pepper if needed.

Note: If cooking in stew or soup, drop, one at a time into gently boiling mixture toward end of cooking time. Stir occasionally; cook for 15 minutes.

Potatoes Romanoff

1 cup Neufchatel cheese dip with bacon and horseradish
1 cup cream-style cottage cheese
2 ounces sharp cheddar cheese, grated
2 tablespoons snipped fresh parsley
1 teaspoon salt
6 cups potatoes, cubed

Cook potatoes until tender. Drain. Combine cheese, cottage cheese, half the shredded cheese, parsley, and salt. Add potatoes; toss gently to coat. Put in a lightly buttered baking dish. Sprinkle with paprika. Bake at 350 degrees, uncovered, for 30 to 35 minutes, or until heated through. Top with remaining shredded cheese; bake 3 to 4 minutes more or until cheese melts.

Rice & Olive Stuffing

Use to stuff dressed fish

1/2 cup butter or margarine
1-1/2 cups onion, minced
2 cups celery, diced
1-1/3 cups cooked wild rice
1-1/3 cups cooked brown rice
1/2 teaspoon salt
1/2 teaspoon pepper
1/2 teaspoon dried sage
1/2 teaspoon dried thyme
2 cups black olives, chopped

Melt butter in a large skillet. Add onion and celery; sauté until tender. Add both kinds of rice and remainder of ingredients. Mix together to blend seasonings evenly throughout mixture.

Variation: Use 2-2/3 cups wild rice; omit brown rice.

Sour Cream Apple Cole Slaw

A little out of the ordinary

1 small head green cabbage, shredded
1 large apple, cored, cubed
2 tablespoons sugar
1/8 teaspoon cinnamon
1/8 teaspoon ground cloves
1/4 teaspoon salt
1/2 cup sour cream
1 teaspoon lemon juice

Combine all ingredients in a large bowl. Toss, blending ingredients thoroughly. Refrigerate and serve.

Sweet and Tangy Carrots

5 cups sliced or diced carrots, cooked
1/2 cup green pepper, chopped
2/3 cup onion, chopped
2/3 cup sugar
1 can (10-3/4-ounce) tomato soup
1/2 cup apple cider vinegar
1/3 cup oil
1 teaspoon Dijon mustard
1 teaspoon Worcestershire sauce

Combine cooked carrots, green pepper, and onion in a large serving bowl. In a medium saucepan, combine remaining ingredients. Bring contents to a boil over medium heat, stirring occasionally. Pour this sauce over vegetables. Refrigerate mixture. Serve cold.

Sweet Potato Chips

A crispy-sweet treat

Sweet Potatoes
Vegetable oil
Sugar or salt

Peel sweet potatoes and slice thin. Heat oil in a heavy skillet, electric skillet or deep fryer. Have oil hot enough for deep-frying. Place slices into oil; fry both sides until golden brown. Remove with a slotted spoon to paper toweling. Sprinkle lightly with either sugar or salt. (Not both) Serve, eat, and enjoy.

Tangy Slaw

6 cups green cabbage, shredded
2 cups red cabbage shredded
1/4 cup onion, finely chopped
1/4 cup red pepper, seeded and chopped
1/4 cup green pepper, seeded and chopped
1/2 cup celery, chopped

Dressing

1/2 cup vegetable oil
1/3 cup vinegar
1/4 cup sugar
1 teaspoon salt
1 teaspoon celery seed
1 teaspoon mustard seed
1/8 teaspoon pepper

In large bowl, combine cabbage, onion, peppers, and celery. In a small bowl or jar, combine all dressing ingredients. Cover; shake well. Pour over cabbage mixture; mix well. Refrigerate at least 1 hour before serving.

Toasted Pumpkin Seeds

Those Halloween Jack-O-Lantern seeds are mighty tasty

Pumpkin seeds, cleaned and washed
3 tablespoons butter or margarine, melted
2 teaspoons soy sauce
1/2 teaspoon Worcestershire
1 teaspoon seasoned salt
1/2 teaspoon garlic powder

Heat oven to 200 degrees. In a bowl, combine all ingredients. Spray a cookie sheet with non-stick spray. Spread mixture out on sheet in a single layer. Bake approximately 1 hour. Turn off oven; leave sheet in oven until cooled completely. Remove and store pumpkin seeds in a covered container.

Twice Baked Sweet Potatoes

Add a sweet surprise to a favorite meal accompaniment

6 medium sweet potatoes
4 tablespoons butter, softened
1 cup chunky applesauce
1 teaspoon pumpkin pie spice
Brown sugar

Wash sweet potatoes; prick with a fork. Place in shallow baking pan; bake at 375 degrees for 45 minutes or until tender. With each potato, cut a thin slice from end to end. Scoop out inside, leaving a thin shell. Place shells in a shallow baking dish.

Mash potatoes; stir in remaining ingredients, except brown sugar. Spoon mixture back into shells; sprinkle with brown sugar. Bake at 375 degrees for 12 to 15 minutes or until heated through.

1-2-3 Meat Marinade

Excellent marinade for kabobs or steaks

1 package (1.12-ounce) dry Meat Marinade
1/4 cup vegetable or canola oil
1/4 cup red wine vinegar
1 large garlic bulb, minced
1/8 cup water
2 to 3 pounds of meat

Using a shallow glass pan or a large plastic zip-top bag, combine marinade mix with oil, wine vinegar, and water. Add meat to marinade and let stand for 15 to 20 minutes. Turn meat several times to absorb flavor. Remove meat from marinade; cook or prepare according to recipe.

Variation: Substitute tarragon wine vinegar, garlic-flavored wine vinegar, or white wine vinegar.

Basic White Sauce

2 tablespoons butter, melted
2 tablespoons all-purpose flour
1 cup milk
1/2 teaspoon salt
1/4 teaspoon white pepper

Combine butter and flour in a saucepan. Add milk slowly, stirring constantly. Cook until thick and smooth. Add salt and pepper. Serve hot.

Cajun Dry Rub

Rub on steaks, roasts, turkey, game bird, or waterfowl

1/2 teaspoon Cajun seasoning
1/4 teaspoon dried rosemary
1/4 teaspoon dried sage
1/4 teaspoon dried thyme
1/2 teaspoon garlic powder
1/2 teaspoon onion powder
3/4 tablespoon seasoned salt

Blend all ingredients in a small bowl. Store mixture in a plastic zip-top bag until ready for use.

Chili Sauce

1 can (28-ounce) diced tomatoes
1 large white onion, chopped
1 large Granny Smith apple, peeled, cored, and chopped
1/2 cup celery, chopped
1/2 cup green pepper, chopped
3/4 cup apple cider vinegar
1-1/2 cups sugar
1/2 teaspoon celery seed
1 teaspoon salt
1/2 teaspoon cinnamon
1/4 teaspoon pepper
1/4 teaspoon nutmeg
1/4 teaspoon ground ginger
Pinch ground cloves
1 tablespoon cornstarch
2 tablespoons water

Combine all ingredients except cornstarch and water in a saucepan. Bring to a boil, reduce heat to simmer and cook gently about 1 hour . Remove, cool and store in a covered container. Refrigerate.

Cooked Herb Marinade

Use with venison, rabbit, or squirrel

1 quart water
1-1/2 cups vinegar
12 whole black peppercorns
1 large onion, chopped
1 carrot, peeled and grated
2 cloves garlic, chopped fine
1 teaspoon fresh, snipped thyme
4 sprigs fresh parsley
1 tablespoon salt

Put all ingredients in saucepan and bring to a boil. Reduce heat to simmer. Cover and simmer for 1 hour. Cool marinade. Use marinade as recipe directs.

Marinade makes enough to cover 5- to 7- pound venison roast.

Cranberry Barbecue Sauce

A basting sauce for wild game

1 cup cranberry juice
1 cup tomato ketchup
1/2 cup water
1/4 cup Worcestershire sauce
1 large tomato, seeded and diced
1/2 green pepper, seeded and chopped
1 tablespoon onion, minced
1 tablespoon prepared horseradish
1-1/2 teaspoons dry mustard

Combine all ingredients in a saucepan. Simmer for 15 minutes. Remove, place in container and refrigerate until ready to use.

Cranberry Ketchup

Excellent served with venison or fowl

2-1/2 pounds cranberries
Vinegar
2-2/3 cups sugar
1 tablespoon cinnamon
1 teaspoon ground cloves

Wash and sort through cranberries; discard any overripe berries. Put cranberries in a saucepan, pour in enough vinegar to cover berries. Cook over medium heat until all cranberries burst open. Remove from heat.

Pour berries and juice through strainer into a bowl. Press berries in strainer to squeeze out remaining juices and pulp. Discard what is left in strainer. Return cranberries to saucepan; stir in sugar, cinnamon, and ground cloves. Simmer until thickened. Pour into container and refrigerate.

Cranberry Sauce for Venison or Fowl

1/2 cup cranberries
1 tablespoon butter or margarine
1-1/4 cups powdered sugar

Wash cranberries. Simmer in a covered saucepan until tender. Watch carefully so as not to burn cranberries. Remove from heat. Purée cranberries in a blender. Cream butter in a bowl, add the cranberry purée and sugar alternately. Beat until smooth. Chill until ready to serve.

Variation: Mash cranberries with a fork or rub through a sieve to produce a puréed effect.

Creamy Mustard Sauce

A welcome addition served with venison steak or roast

1 egg, separated
1 cup whole milk
1 teaspoon quick-mixing flour
1/4 cup sugar
2 tablespoons dry mustard
1/2 teaspoon salt
1/8 teaspoon pepper
1/2 teaspoon dried parsley flakes
2 tablespoons cider vinegar

Beat egg yolk in a small saucepan. Add milk, flour, sugar, mustard, salt, pepper, and parsley. Blend until smooth. Cook over medium heat. Stir constantly until mixture thickens and comes to a boil. Stir in vinegar. Remove from heat. In a bowl, beat egg white until stiff; fold into sauce with spatula. Serve warm.

Cumberland Sauce

A good sauce to serve with duck or goose

1/2 cup orange juice
1/2 cup currant jelly
2 teaspoons lemon juice
1/2 teaspoon grated orange peel
1/8 teaspoon dry mustard
Dash ground cloves
2 tablespoons water
1 tablespoon cornstarch

In saucepan, combine all ingredients except water and cornstarch; heat to boiling. In small bowl, stir together water and cornstarch. Stir into boiling mixture. Continue to cook, stirring constantly until mixture thickens. Serve warm.

Currant Sauce

1 cup currant jelly
1 tablespoon lemon juice
1 teaspoon dry mustard
1/4 teaspoon ground cloves
1/4 teaspoon cinnamon

Combine all ingredients in a small saucepan. Heat, stirring, until currant jelly is dissolved. Serve sauce warm with game.

Easy Mushroom Sauce

Goes well with broiled, baked, or fried fish

1/3 cup onions, sliced
2 tablespoons butter or margarine
1-1/2 cups fresh mushrooms, sliced
1 can (10-3/4-ounce) cream of mushroom soup
1/2 cup milk
1/4 teaspoon dried thyme
Salt and pepper

In a saucepan, melt butter; sauté onions and fresh mushrooms until tender and golden. Gradually stir in soup, then milk. Add seasonings; stir to blend and heat through.

Egg Sauce

Use with fish or game

1/4 cup butter or margarine
1/2 pound fresh mushrooms
5 tablespoons flour
2 cups chicken broth
1/4 cup half-and-half
2 tablespoons dried parsley
1 teaspoon lemon juice
3 hard-cooked egg yolks
Salt and pepper

Melt butter in a saucepan; add mushrooms. Cook 5 minutes, stirring occasionally. Add flour to pan; stir well. Add in broth, stirring to blend. Stir until smooth and thickened. Add half-and-half, parsley, and lemon juice. Press egg yolks through a wire strainer and add into mixture. Salt and pepper to taste.

Flavorful Mushroom Sauce

A delicious sauce over venison steaks

1 tablespoon butter
1/2 cup minced green onions
2-1/2 cups sliced, fresh mushrooms or substitute canned, drained mushrooms
1/2 cup white sherry
1/4 cup brandy
2 cups beef broth
1/8 teaspoon browning sauce (optional)
Flour, quick-mixing (optional)

Melt butter in a sauté pan. Add onions and mushroom; sauté onions until almost tender. Add sherry, brandy, broth and browning sauce; bring to a boil. Reduce heat and simmer for 10 to 15 minutes, reducing liquid to about half the volume. Sauce should not be thick. However, if too thin, sprinkle in a small amount of quick-mixing flour and stir until slightly thickened.

Note: Adjust the amount of sherry and brandy to suit your taste.

Game Wine Marinade

2 cups red or white wine
1/2 cup salad oil
2 medium onions, sliced thin
1 carrot, peeled, finely diced
2 ribs celery, minced
1 clove garlic, minced
1 teaspoon salt
1/4 teaspoon fresh, snipped thyme
2 whole bay leaves
12 whole black peppercorns
2 whole cloves

In a bowl, combine all ingredients and mix well. Use as recipe directs. Makes enough to cover 2 to 3 pounds meat.

Granny's Tartar Sauce

A recipe from the "good ole days"

1 cup mayonnaise
1 tablespoon pickles, chopped, or pickle relish
1 tablespoon stuffed olives, chopped
1 teaspoon parsley, chopped

Combine all ingredients in a container. Refrigerate before serving.

Green Onion Tartar Sauce

1 cup mayonnaise
1 teaspoons green onions, finely minced
2 tablespoons pickle relish
1 teaspoon lemon juice
Dash white pepper

Blend together all ingredients in a bowl. Adjust seasoning, add more lemon juice and/or pepper if needed. Refrigerate. Adjust amount of ingredients to suit your taste.

Herbed Dry Rub

1/4 teaspoon dried rosemary
1/4 teaspoon dried sage
1/4 teaspoon dried thyme
1/2 teaspoon garlic powder
1/2 teaspoon onion powder
1 tablespoon sugar
1 tablespoon black pepper
1 tablespoon seasoned salt

Blend all ingredients well. Store mixture in a plastic zip-top storage bag until ready for use.

Rub on turkey, game bird, or fowl before cooking.

Hoisin Peanut Dipping Sauce

1/2 cup chicken broth
2 tablespoons hoisin sauce
2 tablespoons sesame oil
2 tablespoons soy sauce
1 tablespoon creamy peanut butter
1 teaspoon cornstarch

Bring all ingredients to a boil in a small saucepan, stirring; boil 1 minute. Refrigerate until ready to use. Reheat and serve.

Homemade Tartar Sauce

1 cup mayonnaise
2 tablespoons sweet pickles, chopped fine
1 teaspoon minced onion
1 teaspoon lemon juice
1 teaspoon parsley, chopped
1 teaspoon tarragon

Blend together all ingredients in a container. Adjust the amount of ingredients to suit your taste. Refrigerate until ready to use.

Honey Dipping Sauce

2 tablespoons cornstarch
1 cup water, divided
1/2 cup honey
1/4 cup prepared mustard

In a small saucepan, dissolve cornstarch in 1 tablespoon water. Add honey, mustard and remaining water. Bring to a boil. Boil for 1 minute, stirring constantly. Serve.

Honey Mustard Sauce

Serve with fish or game

1/2 cup plain yogurt
4 teaspoons Dijon mustard
4 teaspoons honey
1 tablespoon dried dill
2 teaspoons white-wine vinegar
1/2 teaspoon sugar
1/8 teaspoon ground white pepper

In a small bowl, blend all ingredients with a whisk or fork. Cover and refrigerate 2 hours. Before serving sauce, whisk again.

Mustard Fruits

Old-fashioned fruity meat sauce

1 cup Sauterne wine
1 cup water
1/2 cup sugar
4 pears, peeled, cored and diced
1/2 cup bite-sized pitted prunes, diced
1/2 cup dried apricot halves, diced
1/4 cup dried cranberries (craisins)
4 to 6 tablespoons Dijon mustard

In a medium skillet, combine wine, water and sugar; bring to a boil. Add all fruit. Simmer until pears are tender. Remove fruit with a slotted spoon. Increase heat; reduce pan juices to 1/2 cup and until sugars have begun to caramelize. Blend in 4 tablespoons of mustard. Add more mustard if desired, according to taste. Return fruit to skillet; stir gently to blend with sauce. Keep warm until ready to serve.

Serve with pheasant, partridge, turkey, or rabbit.

Old Fashioned Cheese Sauce

2 tablespoons melted butter or margarine
2 tablespoons all-purpose flour
1 cup milk
1 egg yolk, well beaten
1/8 teaspoon pepper
3/4 teaspoon salt
2 tablespoons grated cheese of your choice
Dash of paprika

Use a very low temperature to slowly melt butter in a small saucepan. Stir flour into melted butter; pour in milk slowly, stirring constantly. Cook until thick and smooth, stirring constantly. Slowly pour in egg yolk, stirring constantly. Add salt and pepper, seasoning to taste. Add cheese, stir to melt; blend in with sauce.

Serve cheese sauce with baked or grilled fish, fish loaf, or vegetables. Add a dash of paprika as a bit of color on top of sauce.

Onion Velvet Sauce

Perfect sauce for upland or small game

2 tablespoons minced green onions and tops
2 tablespoons butter or margarine
2 tablespoons quick mixing flour
3/4 cup chicken broth
1/4 cup half-and-half
1/8 teaspoon poultry seasoning

Melt butter over low heat in a saucepan. Add onion, cook for 2 minutes. Stir in flour. Blend in chicken broth, half-and-half, and poultry seasoning. Cook, stirring constantly, until sauce has thickened. Adjust seasoning if needed. Serve warm.

Poultry Dry Rub

3/4 cup paprika
1/8 cup crushed black peppercorns
1/8 cup salt
1/2 cup dried parsley leaves
1/2 cup dried basil leaves
1/2 cup dried thyme leaves
1/2 cup dried rosemary leaves

Blend all ingredients in a bowl and mix together well. Crush larger pieces so everything is a uniform consistency. Store in an airtight container in a cool, dark, dry place. Freeze what you don't plan to use.

Pepper Marinade for Game

1 medium onion, chopped fine
2 carrots, diced
1 small rib celery, chopped fine
1/4 cup olive oil
3-1/2 cups dry red wine
3/4 cup cider vinegar
3/4 teaspoon black peppercorns
1 whole clove
1 bay leaf, crushed
1/2 teaspoon thyme
1/2 teaspoon marjoram
1 teaspoon salt

Sauté onion, carrots, and celery in oil until tender, but not browned. Add remaining ingredients. Bring to a boil and simmer 20 minutes. Cool completely before using.

To use marinade, place game in a bowl; pour cooled marinade over game and let stand in refrigerator two to five days. Turn meat two or three times a day. Drain meat and pat dry before preparing in recipe.

Port Wine Sauce

1 cup port wine
1/2 cup orange juice
2 shallots, sliced
1 sprig fresh thyme or 1/8 teaspoon dry thyme
1 cup chicken broth
2 teaspoons cornstarch
Salt and pepper
1 medium orange, peeled and sectioned
Grated orange rind

Pour wine and orange juice into a small saucepan. Add shallots and thyme; simmer. When the liquid has been reduced to half its volume, add chicken broth and stir.

In a small bowl, mix cornstarch with a little orange juice or water. Slowly stir into simmering liquid, cook until sauce has thickened. Add orange sections and rind; season with salt and pepper to taste.

Red Raisin Sauce

1 jar (10-ounce) red currant jelly
1/2 cup golden raisins
1/4 cup butter or margarine
2 teaspoons lemon juice
1/4 teaspoon ground allspice

In a medium-sized saucepan, combine all ingredients. Cook over medium-low heat, stirring occasionally until blended, about 10 minutes.

Use as a basting sauce for roasted pheasant, partridge, or turkey, or as a sauce served on the side.

Red Wine & Herb Marinade

Fresh herbs from the garden enhance this marinade

4 cups dry red wine
1/4 cup celery leaves, coarsely chopped
3 peppercorns
3 whole cloves
1 whole bay leaf
A few sprigs each of thyme and parsley, coarsely chopped
Salt to taste

Mix all ingredients in bowl. Add meat and marinate 24 hours in refrigerator before cooking. Turn meat occasionally during marinating process.

Red Wine Marinade

Use this recipe for marinating venison steaks or chops.

1 cup dry red wine
2 cups water
1/4 teaspoon thyme
2 whole bay leaves
1 cup onion, coarsely chopped
1 garlic clove, minced fine
1/2 teaspoon fresh ground black pepper

Combine all ingredients in mixing bowl, stirring well. Add venison and moisten thoroughly with marinade. Place in refrigerator, turning occasionally. Marinate meat for 4 hours before cooking.

Spicy Tomato Sauce

Serve with any wild game, fish, or vegetable

1 cup canned, diced tomatoes
1/2 cup water
2 whole cloves
1/8 teaspoon celery salt
1/2 tablespoon parsley, minced
1/2 tablespoon onion, minced
1 whole bay leaf
2 tablespoons butter, melted
2 tablespoons quick-mixing flour
Salt and pepper
Dash or two of liquid hot sauce

Combine tomatoes, water, clove, celery salt, parsley, onion, and bay leaf in a saucepan. Cover. Simmer for 10 minutes. Remove bay leaf and clove from mixture. Add butter and sprinkle in flour, stirring constantly until smooth and desired thickness. Season with salt, pepper and liquid hot sauce to taste.

Sweet-Tangy Mustard Sauce

1 cup half-and-half
1 egg yolk, beaten
1/2 cup sugar
4 teaspoons all-purpose flour
5 teaspoons dry mustard
1/8 teaspoon salt
1/3 cup vinegar

In a small bowl, combine half-and-half and egg yolk; set aside. In a small sauce-pan, combine sugar, flour, dry mustard, and salt. Use a wire whisk to gradually stir in half-and-half mixture. Cook over medium heat, stirring constantly, until sauce is thickened. Remove from heat; stir in vinegar. Serve warm or cold.

Tip: Store in refrigerator in covered container for up to 4 weeks.

Tomato Sauce

Serve with wild game, fish, or vegetables

2 cups canned tomato soup
1 teaspoon green pepper, chopped
1 teaspoon onion, chopped
1 teaspoon butter or margarine
Salt and pepper

Heat tomato soup to boiling. Add onion, green pepper, and butter. Season to taste. Simmer 5 minutes.

Uncooked Oil-Based Marinade

Use this simple marinade for steaks and chops

1 cup canola oil
2 cups dry vermouth
1 onion, sliced in thin rings
1 lemon, sliced in thin rings
1 whole bay leaf
2 tablespoons brown sugar
6 peppercorns, crushed
3 tablespoons fresh rosemary leaves, chopped

Mix all ingredients in a bowl or plastic zip-top bag. Add meat, cover and refrigerate 24 hours before cooking.

Wild Duck Sauce

A delicious accompaniment spooned over roast duck

1/4 cup red currant jelly
3 tablespoons butter
2 tablespoons dry sherry
Salt and pepper
Lemon juice

Using a small saucepan, melt jelly over very low heat. Stir, being careful that jelly does not scorch. Add butter, sherry, salt and pepper, stir to blend. Blend in enough lemon juice to make the sauce tart enough to suit your taste. Serve on the side with roast duck.

Zesty Fish Sauce

1 cup mayonnaise
1/4 cup French dressing
1/4 cup chili sauce
1 teaspoon horseradish
1 teaspoon Worcestershire
Salt and coarse ground pepper

Combine the first 5 ingredients. Add salt and pepper to taste. Refrigerate until ready to serve.

Serve with broiled, pan-fried, or oven-fried fish.

Blackberry Summer Pie

A berry easy, tasty favorite for family and friends

Crust: 1 piecrust from (15-ounce) package refrigerated piecrusts

Cream Cheese Layer:
1 package (3-ounce) cream cheese, softened
2 tablespoons powdered sugar
1-1/2 tablespoons milk

Berry Mixture:
3/4 cups sugar
2-1/2 tablespoons cornstarch
1/4 teaspoon salt
2/3 cups water
4 cups fresh blackberries
2 tablespoons butter or margarine

Fit 1 piecrust into a 9-inch pie plate according to package directions. Bake as directed on package for a fruit pie.

Mix cream cheese and powdered sugar in a small bowl. Add milk a little at a time, mixing until a smooth consistency. Spread mixture in bottom of baked piecrust and refrigerate.

In a 2 quart saucepan, combine sugar, cornstarch and salt. Stir in water and 1 cup of berries. Cook at medium heat, stirring constantly until thick, about 5 to 7 minutes. Crush berries against the side of pan with a spoon until they are completely crushed. Remove pan from heat, stir in 2 tablespoons butter. Set mixture aside to cool. When cooled, gently fold in remaining 3 cups blackberries. Carefully spoon and spread berry mixture onto cheese layer. Refrigerate and chill for hour.

Serve pie with either a large dollop of whipped cream or a generous portion of vanilla ice cream.

Corn Fritters

2 cups canned corn, drained
1 teaspoon salt
1/8 teaspoon pepper
1 egg
1 teaspoon butter, melted
1/2 cup milk
2 cups flour
1 teaspoon baking powder

Combine all ingredients in a bowl. Mix well. Heat vegetable oil to 375 degrees.
Drop batter by spoonfuls into hot oil. When golden brown, remove, drain on
paper toweling, and serve.

Cranberry Ice

A cool delight

4 cups cranberries
2 cups water
2 cups sugar
Juice of 2 lemons

Cook cranberries and water together in a saucepan for 10 minutes. Remove
from heat and force through a sieve into a bowl. To the cranberry mixture, add
sugar and juice from the lemons. Stir to mix. Place in a container and freeze to a
mush-like consistency. Serve.

Cranberry Streusel Pie

A sweet and tangy Wisconsin treat

1 piecrust from (15-ounce) package refrigerated piecrusts
2 cups cranberries, fresh or frozen
1/2 cup chopped walnuts
1/2 teaspoon ground cinnamon
1/4 cup white sugar
1/4 cup firmly packed light brown sugar
1 large egg
1/8 teaspoon nutmeg
1/4 cup butter, melted
1/2 cup sugar
3 tablespoons all-purpose flour

Fit piecrust into a 9-inch pie plate, according to package directions. Fold edges under and crimp. In a bowl, combine cranberries, walnuts, cinnamon and sugars. Spoon into piecrust. Mix together the egg and remaining ingredients. Pour over cranberry mixture.

Bake at 400 degrees for 20 minutes. Reduce temperature to 350 degrees, bake for an additional 30 minutes. Serve with whipped cream or ice cream.

Decadent Brandied Cranberry Apples

1-1/2 cups brandy
1-1/2 cups apple cider
6 large Granny Smith apples
5 tablespoons brown sugar
6 tablespoons dried cranberries (craisens)
1/2 teaspoon ground cinnamon
2 tablespoons butter, cut up

Combine brandy and apple cider in a saucepan; bring to a boil. Reduce heat to a gentle boil and cook about 30 to 40 minutes until liquid is reduced to 1 cup.

Core apples and place in a lightly buttered baking dish. Fill each apple cavity with 2 teaspoons brown sugar and 1 tablespoon cranberries. Pour brandy mixture over apples.

Combine remaining 1 tablespoon brown sugar and cinnamon; sprinkle mixture evenly over apples. Dot each apple with butter. Cover and bake at 350 degrees for 15 minutes. Uncover and bake 15 more minutes or until tender. Baste apples occasionally with juice from bottom of pan. Serve with vanilla ice cream.

Variation: Substitute 1-1/2 cups apple cider for brandy (bringing the total to 3 cups apple cider) if desired.

Farmhouse Maple-Sugar Cake

Adapted from an old handwritten recipe

1/2 cup butter or shortening
1-1/4 cups maple sugar
1-1/4 teaspoons vanilla
6 tablespoons cornstarch
1-1/2 cups all-purpose flour
1/2 cup milk
4 egg whites

In a bowl, cream butter or shortening and sugar. Add vanilla and mix. Sift cornstarch and flour together two times into a bowl. Third time, sift into creamed butter mixture alternately with the milk. Stir and mix. Beat egg whites until stiff with electric beater. Fold in the stiffly beaten egg whites into cake mixture. Pour cake mixture in a greased loaf-cake pan. Bake at 375 degrees for 50 minutes or until a toothpick comes out clean when poked into center of cake. Cover with any desired icing.

Fruit Stuffed Baked Apples

An old time favorite dessert updated

6 large tart red apples
3/4 cup bananas, chopped
3/4 cup cranberries, coarsely chopped
1 cup sugar
1 teaspoon cinnamon
1/4 teaspoon nutmeg
Walnuts or pecans, chopped
Ice cream or whipped cream

Cut off small amount of apple bottom to flatten. Cut off stem end of the apples, but do not peel them. Remove the entire core and some of the pulp, leaving the walls of the apple about 1/2 to 3/4 inch thick. Mix apple pulp, bananas, cranberries, sugar, cinnamon and nutmeg. Fill apple cavities with this mixture. Cover with chopped walnuts or pecans. Bake at 325 degrees until tender. Cool slightly. Serve with a spoonful of vanilla ice cream or whipped cream sprinkled with nutmeg on top of each apple.

Rhubarb Custard Pie

"Pieplant" at it's best

4 cups fresh rhubarb cut into 1/2 inch pieces
1 piecrust from (15-ounce) package refrigerated piecrusts
1 cup sugar
1 tablespoon all-purpose flour
1/4 teaspoon ground nutmeg
4 eggs, slightly beaten

Fit 1 piecrust into a 9-inch pie plate according to package directions. Place rhubarb in pastry shell. Combine sugar, flour, and nutmeg. Add eggs; beat well. Pour egg mixture into pastry shell.

To prevent overbrowning, cover edge with foil. Bake in a 375-degree oven 25 minutes. Remove foil; bake 20 minutes more or until pie is nearly set (pie appears soft in center, but sets upon cooling). Cool. Cover and store in refrigerator.

Wild Raspberry Fritters

A berry tasty treat

3 eggs
1 cup all-purpose flour
1 teaspoon baking powder
1 teaspoon salt
1/2 cup water
2 cups raspberries
vegetable oil
powdered sugar

Separate egg yolks from the whites. Sift flour, baking powder and salt into a bowl. Beat egg yolks, add to flour mixture along with water. In a separate bowl, beat raspberries with mixer until broken down. In another bowl, beat egg whites to a stiff froth; fold into batter. Fold in the raspberries. Heat oil to 375 degrees. Drop batter by spoonfuls into hot oil. When golden brown, remove and drain on paper toweling. Dust with powdered sugar.

Wild Raspberry Pudding Pie

You won't get the raspberries from anyone, when you serve this pie

1 9-inch piecrust, baked
1 package (3-ounce) vanilla pudding mix (NOT instant)
1-1/2 cups milk
1/4 teaspoon almond extract
1 cup whipped cream
3 cups raspberries
1/2 cup water
1 tablespoon sugar
1 tablespoon cornstarch
1 teaspoon lemon zest
1 tablespoon lemon juice

Prepare pudding using only 1-1/2 cups of milk. Stir in the almond extract. Cover and refrigerate mixture for one hour. Fold whipped cream into pudding. Spoon mixture into baked piecrust. Refrigerate.

Pick over the berries, set aside 2 cups of the best ones. In a medium saucepan, add 1 cup of berries, 1/2 cup water, sugar, cornstarch, lemon zest, and lemon juice. Stir mixture over medium heat until it thickens. Remove pan from heat; cool. Carefully fold in remaining 2 cups raspberries. Spoon berry mixture over pudding in the pie shell. Refrigerate for about 4 hours.

Index

O

P

S

W